Naval Engineering Plants
(1955 - 1990)

Naval Engineering Plants (1955 - 1990)

Gregory Collins

authorHOUSE®

AuthorHouse™
1663 Liberty Drive
Bloomington, IN 47403
www.authorhouse.com
Phone: 1-800-839-8640

Published by AuthorHouse 10/9/12

ISBN: 978-1-4772-7850-5 (sc)
ISBN: 978-1-4772-7849-9 (e)

Acknowledgment

The information contained herein has been adapted from the *Principles of Naval Engineering*, prepared by the Bureau of Naval Personnel, NAVPERS 10788-B, First edition 1958, revised 1966, 1970; U.S. Government Printing Office Washington, D.C. 20402. The majority of this text was prepared by the Training Publications Division, Naval Personnel Program Support Activity, Washington, D.C. To the extent, this book may contain text in the public domain; the Author makes no claim of ownership. The Author is credited for text compilation and editing. United States Navy photographs taken by Julia A. Casper, Andrew K. Haller, Kyle Steckler and Patrick L. Heil and released to the public.

Contents

Introduction

N*aval Engineering Plants (1955 - 1990)* provides an introduction to the theory and design of engineering machinery and equipment aboard naval ships. The fundamentals of shipboard machinery, equipment, and engineering plants are presented and compiled for engineering professionals. Primary emphasis is placed on helping the reader acquire a historical view of shipboard engineering plants and an understanding of basic theoretical considerations that underlie the design of machinery and equipment. Official illustrations and details of operation, maintenance, and repair are not included in this text. The text is divided into three major parts. Part I deals with certain theoretical considerations that apply to virtually all engineering equipment are discussed. Part II takes up the major units of machinery in the main propulsion cycle of the then widely used steam turbine propulsion plant. Other types of propulsion machinery, together with a brief survey of new developments in naval engineering, are considered in part III. In addition to these three major parts, the text includes a number of references that should be of value to engineering professionals.

Part I discusses: Basic Engineering Theory. We cannot proceed very far in the study of naval engineering plants without realizing the need for basic theoretical knowledge in many areas. To understand the functioning of the machinery and equipment discussed in later parts of this text, we must know something of the principles of mechanics, the laws of motion, the structure of matter, the behavior of molecules and atoms and subatomic particles, the properties and behavior of solids, liquids, gases, and other principles and concepts derived from the physical sciences. Chapter 1 takes up the fundamentals of resistance, the development and transmission of propulsive power, and the principles of steering. Theoretical considerations of a more specialized nature are discussed in other chapters throughout the text, as they are required for an understanding of the particular machinery or equipment under discussion.

Part II discusses: The Conventional Steam Turbine Propulsion Plant. This part of the text deals with the major units of machinery in the conventional steam turbine propulsion plant-a type of plant, which is at present widely used in naval ships. For the most part, the discussion is concerned with geared-turbine drive; but some of the information is also applicable to those few ships with turboelectric drive. The term "conventional" is used here to indicate that the plants under discussion utilize conventional boilers, rather than nuclear reactors, as the source of heat for the generation of steam. Chapter 2 deals with propulsion boilers and their fittings and Controls.

Part III discusses: Other Types of Propulsion Plants. The conventional steam turbine propulsion plant, although widely used, was by no means the only propulsion plant in naval use. Chapter 3 deals with internal combustion engines of the reciprocating type— diesel and gasoline. Chapter 4 discusses the increasingly important gas turbine engine. Chapter 5 discusses the nuclear power plant—a plant which utilizes the steam turbine as a prime mover but employs the nuclear reactor rather than the conventional boiler as a source of heat for the generation of steam.

CHAPTER 1

SHIP PROPULSION AND STEERING

The ability to move through the water and the ability to control the direction of movement are among the most fundamental of all ship requirements. Ship propulsion is achieved through the conversion, transmission, and utilization of energy in a sequence of events that includes the development of power in a prime mover, transmission of power to the propellers, development of thrust on the working surfaces of the propeller blades, and the transmission of thrust to the ship's structure in such a way as to move the ship through the water. Control of the direction of movement is achieved partially by steering devices, which receive their power from steering engines and partially by the arrangement, speed, and direction of rotation of the ship's propellers.

This chapter is concerned with basic principles of ship propulsion and steering and with the propellers, bearings, shafting, reduction gears, rudders, and other devices required to move the ship and to control its direction of movement. The prime movers which are the source of propulsive power are discussed in detail in other chapters of this text, and are therefore mentioned only briefly in this chapter.

Resistance

The movement of a ship through the water requires the expenditure of sufficient energy to overcome the resistance of the water and, to a lesser extent, the resistance of the air. The components of resistance may be considered as (1) skin or frictional resistance, (2) wave-making resistance, (3) eddy resistance, and (4) air resistance.

Skin or *frictional resistance* occurs because liquid particles in contact with the ship are carried along with the ship, while liquid particles a short distance away are moving at much lower velocities. Frictional resistance is therefore the result of fluid shear between adjacent layers of water. Under most conditions, frictional resistance constitutes a large part of the total resistance.

Wave-making resistance results from the generation and propagation of wave trains by the ship in motion. When the crests of the waves make an oblique angle with the line of the ship's direction, the waves are known as *diverging waves.* These waves, once generated, travel clear of the ship and give no further trouble. The *transverse waves,* which have a crest line at a 90° angle to the ship's direction, do not have visible, breaking crests. The transverse waves are actually the invisible part of the continuous wave train, which includes the visible divergent waves at the bow and stern. The wave-making resistance of the ship is a resistance that must be allowed for in the design of ships, since the generation and propagation of wave trains requires the expenditure of a definite amount of energy.

Eddy resistance occurs when the flow lines do not close in behind a moving hull, thus creating a low-pressure area in the water behind the stern of the ship. Because of this low-pressure area, energy is dissipated as the water eddies. Most ships are designed to minimize the separation of the flow lines from the ship, thus minimizing eddy resistance. Eddy resistance is relatively minor in naval ships.

Air resistance, although small, also requires the expenditure of some energy. Air resistance may be considered as frictional resistance and eddy resistance, with most of it being eddy resistance.

The Development and Transmission of Propulsive Power

The geared-turbine installation is the propulsion plant most commonly used in naval service during 1955 through 1990. The basic principles of this installation starts with the high and low-pressure turbines, thrust bearing, main reduction gear, line shaft bearings, main shaft, stern tube bearing, strut, strut bearing, and propeller.

The same basic principles apply to all types of propulsion plants.

The units directly involved in the development and transmission of propulsive power are the prime mover, the shaft, the propelling device, and the thrust bearing. The various bearings used to support the shaft

4

and the reduction gears (in this installation) may be regarded as necessary accessories.

The *prime mover* provides the mechanical energy required to turn the shaft and drive the propelling device. The steam turbines constitute the prime mover of this installation; in other installations, the prime mover may be a diesel engine, a gas turbine engine, or a turbine-driven generator.

The *propulsion shaft* provides a means of transmitting mechanical energy from the prime mover to the propelling device and transmitting thrust from the propelling device to the thrust bearing.

The *propelling device* imparts velocity to a column of water and moves it in the direction *opposite* to the direction in which it is desired to move the ship. A reactive force (thrust) is thereby developed against the velocity-imparting device; and this thrust, when transmitted to the ship's structure, causes the ship to move through the water. Fundamentally, we may think of propelling devices as pumps, which are designed to move a column of water in order to build up a reactive force sufficient to move the ship. The screw propeller is the propelling device used on practically all naval ships.

The *thrust bearing* absorbs the axial thrust that is developed on the propeller and transmitted through the shaft. Since the thrust bearing is firmly fixed in relation to the ship's structure, any thrust developed on the propeller must be transmitted to the ship in such a way as to move the ship through the water.

The purpose of the *bearings* that support the shaft is to absorb radial thrust and to maintain the correct alignment of the shaft and the propeller.

The *reduction gears* are used to allow the turbines to operate at high rotational speed while the propellers operate at lower speeds, thus providing for most efficient operation of both turbines and propellers.

The propellers, bearings, shafting, and reduction gears which are directly or indirectly involved in the development and transmission of propulsive power are considered in more detail following a general discussion of power requirements for naval ships.

Power Requirements

The power output of a marine engine is expressed in terms of horsepower. One horsepower is equal to 550 foot-pounds of work per second or 33,000 foot-pounds of work per minute. Different types of engines are rated in different kinds of horsepower. Steam reciprocating engines are rated in terms of indicated horsepower (ihp); internal combustion engines are usually rated in terms of brake horsepower (bhp); and steam turbines are rated in terms of shaft horsepower (shp).

Indicated horsepower is the power measured in the cylinders of the engine. *Brake horsepower* is the power measured at the crankshaft coupling by means of a mechanical, hydraulic, or electric brake. *Shaft horsepower* is the power transmitted through the shaft to the propeller. Shaft horsepower can be measured with a torsion meter. It can also be determined by computation. Shaft horsepower may vary from time to time within the same plant because of variations in the condition of the bottom, the draft of the ship, the state of the sea, and other factors. Shaft horsepower may be determined by the following formula:

$$shp = \frac{2\pi\,NT}{33,000}$$

Where

shp = shaft horsepower
N = rpm
T = torque (in foot-pounds) measured with a torsion meter

The amount of power, which the propelling machinery must develop in order to drive a ship at a desired speed, may be determined by direct calculation or by calculations based on the measured resistance of a model having a definite size relationship to the ship.

When the latter method of calculating power requirements is used, ship models are towed at various speeds in long tanks or basins. The most elaborate facility for testing models in this way was the Navy's David W. Taylor Model Basin at Carderock, Maryland. The main basin was 2,775 feet long, 51 feet wide and 22 feet deep. A powered carriage spanning this tank and riding on machine rails was equipped to tow an attached model directly below it. The carriages carried instruments to measure and record the speed of travel and the resistance of the model. From the resistance, the effective horsepower (ehp) (among other things) could have been calculated. Effective horsepower is the horsepower required to tow the ship. Therefore,

$$ehp = \dfrac{\dfrac{6080V}{R_T\,60}}{33,000}$$

Where

  ehp = effective horsepower
  R_T = tow rope resistance, in pounds
  V = speed, in knots

The speed in knots is multiplied by 6,080 to convert it to feet per hour, and is divided by 60 to convert this to feet per minute.

The relationship between effective horsepower and shaft horsepower is called the *propulsive efficiency* or the propulsive coefficient of the ship. It is equal to the product of the propeller efficiency and the hull efficiency.

The variation of hull resistance at moderate speeds of any well-designed ship is approximately proportional to the square of the speed. The power required to propel a ship is proportional to the product of the hull resistance and speed. Therefore, it follows that under steady running conditions, the power required to drive a ship is approximately proportional to the cube of propeller speed. While this relationship is not exact enough for actual design, it does serve as a useful guide for operating the propelling plant.

Since the power required to drive a ship is approximately proportional to the cube of the propeller speed, 50 percent of full power will drive a ship at about 79.4 percent of the maximum speed attainable when full power is used for propulsion, and only 12.5 percent of full power is needed for about 50 percent of maximum speed attained.

The relation of speed, torque, and horsepower to ship's resistance and propeller speed under steady running conditions can be expressed in the following equations:

$S = k_1 \times (rpm)$

$$T = k_2 \times (rpm)^2$$

$$shp = \frac{2\pi \, k_2 \times (rpm)^3}{33,000}$$

Where

S = ship's speed, in knots
T = torque required to turn propeller, in foot-pounds
shp = shaft horsepower
rpm = propeller revolutions per minute
k_1, k_2 = proportionality factors

The proportionality factors depend on many conditions such as displacement, trim, condition of hull and propeller with respect to fouling, depth of water, sea and wind conditions, and the position of the ship. Conditions that increase the resistance of the ship to motion, cause k_1 to be smaller and k_2 to be larger.

In a smooth sea, the proportionality factors k_1 and k_2 can be considered as being reasonably constant. However, in rough seas a ship is subjected to varying degrees of immersion and wave impact, which cause these factors to fluctuate over a considerable range. Therefore, it is to be expected that peak loads in excess of the loads required in smooth seas will be imposed on the propulsion plant to maintain the ship's rated speed. Propulsion plants are designed with sufficient reserve power to handle the fluctuating loads that must be expected.

There is no simple relationship for determining the power required to reverse the propeller when the ship is moving ahead or the power required to turn the propeller ahead when the ship is moving astern. To meet Navy requirements, a ship must be able to reverse from full speed ahead to full speed astern within a prescribed period of time; the propulsion plant of any ship must be designed to furnish sufficient power for meeting the reversing specifications.

Propellers

The propelling device most commonly used for naval ships is the screw propeller, so called because it advances through the water in somewhat the same way that a screw advances through wood or a bolt advances when it is screwed into a nut. With the screw propeller, as with a screw, the axial distance advanced with each complete revolution is known as the *pitch*. The path of advance of each propeller blade section is approximately helicoidal (a flatten spiral-shape).

However, there is a difference between the way a screw propeller advances and the way a bolt advances in a nut. Since water is not a solid medium, the propeller slips or skids; hence the actual distance advanced in one complete revolution is less than the theoretical advance for one complete revolution. The difference between the theoretical and the actual advance per revolution is called the *slip*. Slip is usually expressed as a ratio of the theoretical advance per revolution (or, in other words, the pitch) and the actual advance per revolution. Thus,

$$\text{Slip ratio} = \frac{E - A}{E}$$

Where

E = shaft rpm x pitch = engine distance per minute
A = actual distance advanced per minute

Screw propellers may be broadly classified as *fixed pitch propellers* or *controllable pitch propellers*. The pitch of a fixed pitch propeller cannot be altered during operation; the pitch of a controllable pitch propeller can be changed continuously, subject to bridge or engine-room control. Most propellers in naval use during 1955 through 1990 are of the fixed pitch type, but some controllable pitch propellers were in service.

A screw propeller consists of a hub and several (usually three or four) blades spaced at equal angles about the axis. Where the blades are integral with the hub, the propeller is known as a *solid propeller*. Where the blades are separately cast and secured to the hub by means of studs and nuts, the propeller is referred to as a *built-up propeller*.

Solid propellers may be further classified as having *constant pitch* or *variable pitch*. In a constant pitch propeller, the pitch of each radius is the same. On a variable pitch propeller, the pitch at each radius may vary. Solid propellers of the variable pitch type were the most commonly used for naval ships from 1955 through 1990.

Propellers are classified as being *right-hand* or *left-hand* propellers, depending upon the direction of rotation. When viewed from astern, with the ship moving ahead, a right-hand propeller rotates in a clockwise direction and a left-hand propeller rotates in a counterclockwise direction. The great majority of single-screw ships have right-hand propellers. Multiple-screw ships have right hand propellers to port. Reversing the direction of rotation of a propeller reverses the direction of thrust and consequently reverses the direction of the ship's movement.

There are terms used in connection with screw propellers. The term *face* (or pressure face) identifies the after side of the blade, when the ship is moving ahead. The term *back* (or *suction back*) identifies the surface opposite the face. As the propeller rotates, the face of the blade increases the pressure on the water near it and gives the water a positive astern movement. The back of the blade creates a low-pressure or suction area just ahead of the blade. The overall thrust is derived from the increased water velocity, which results from the total pressure differential thus created.

The *tip* of the blade is the point most distant from the hub. The *root* of the blade is the area where the blade arm joins the hub. The *leading edge* is the edge, which first cuts the water when the ship is going ahead. The *trailing edge* (also called the *following edge*) is opposite the leading edge. A *rake angle* exists when there is a rake either forward or aft—that is, when the blade is not precisely perpendicular to the long axis of the shaft.

Blade Angle

The blade angle (or pitch angle) of a propeller may be defined as the angle included between the blade and a line perpendicular to the shaft centerline. If the blade angle were 0°, no pressure would be developed on the blade face. If the blade angle were 90°, the entire pressure would be exerted sidewise and none of it aft. Within certain limits, the amount of reactive thrust developed by a blade is a function of the blade angle.

Blade Velocity

The sternward velocity imparted to the water by the rotation of the propeller blades is partially a function of the speed at which the blades rotate. In general, the higher the speed, the greater the reactive thrust.

However, not every part of a rotating blade gives equal velocity to the water unless the blade is specially designed to do this. For example, on a flat blade with two points, the two points move about the shaft center with equal angular velocity (rpm) but with different instantaneous linear velocities. One point must move farther than the other point to complete one revolution; hence, the linear velocity at one point must be greater than at the other point. With the same pitch angle, therefore, one point will exert more pressure on the water and so develop more reactive thrust than the other point. The higher the linear velocity of any part of a blade, the greater will be the reactive thrust.

Real propeller blades are not flat but are designed with complex surfaces (approximately helicoidal) to permit every infinitesimal area to produce equal thrust. There is a top, middle and bottom point. Since one point has a higher linear velocity than the bottom point, the thrust at the top point must be decreased by decreasing the pitch angle at the top point. The middle point would have (on a flat blade) a linear velocity less than the top but greater than the bottom points. In a real propeller, the middle point must be set at a pitch angle, which is greater than the pitch angle at the top point but less than the pitch angle at the bottom point. Since the linear velocity of the parts of a blade varies from root to tip, and since it is desired to have every infinitesimal area of the blade produce equal thrust, it is apparent that a real propeller must vary the pitch angle from root to tip.

Propeller Size

The size of a propeller— that is, the size of the area swept by the blades—has a definite effect on the total thrust that can be developed on the propeller. Within certain limits, the thrust that can be developed increases as the diameter and the total blade area increase. Since it is impracticable to increase propeller diameter beyond a certain point, propeller blade area is usually made as great as possible by using as many blades as are feasible under the circumstances. Three-bladed and four-bladed marine propellers were commonly used.

Thrust Deduction

Because of the friction between the hull and the water, water is carried forward with the hull and is given a forward velocity. This movement of adjacent water is called the *wake*. Since the propeller revolves in this body of forward moving water, the sternward velocity given to the propeller is less than if there were no wake. Since the wake is traveling with the ship, the speed of advance over the ground is greater than the speed through the wake.

At the same time, a propeller draws water from under the stern of the ship, creating a suction, which tends to keep the ship from going ahead. The increase in resistance that occurs because of this suction is known as thrust deduction.

Number and Location of Propellers

A single propeller is located on the ship's centerline as far aft as possible to minimize the thrust deduction factor. Vertically, the propeller must be located deep enough so that instill water the blades do not draw in air but high enough so that it can benefit from the wake. The propeller must not be located so high that it will be likely to break the surface in rough weather, since this would lead to racing and perhaps a broken shaft.

A twin-screw ship had the propellers located one on each side, well aft, with sufficient tip clearance to limit thrust deduction.

A quadruple-screw ship had the outboard propellers located forward of and above the inboard propellers, to avoid propeller stream interference.

Controllable Pitch Propellers

As previously noted, controllable pitch propellers were in use on some naval ships. Controllable pitch propellers gave a ship excellent maneuverability and allowed the propellers to develop maximum thrust at any given engine rpm.

A ship with controllable pitch propellers requires much less distance for stopping than a ship with fixed pitch propellers. The controllable pitch propellers are particularly useful for landing ships because they make it possible for the ships to hover offshore and because they make it easier for the ships to retract and turn away from the beach.

Controllable pitch propellers may be controlled from the bridge or from the engine-room. Hydraulic or mechanical controls are used to apply a blade actuating force to the blades.

A hydraulic system is the most widely used means of providing the force required to change the pitch of a controllable pitch propeller. In this type of system, a valve positioning mechanism actuates an oil control valve. The oil control valve permits hydraulic oil, under pressure, to be introduced to either side of a piston (which is connected to the propeller blade) and at the same time allows for the controlled discharge of hydraulic oil from the other side of the piston. This action repositions the piston and thus changes the pitch of the propeller blades.

Some controllable pitch propellers have mechanical means for providing the blade actuating force necessary to change the pitch of the blades. In these designs, a worm screw and crosshead nut are used instead of the hydraulic devices for transmitting the actuating force to the connecting rods. The torque required for rotating the worm screw is supplied either by an electric motor or by the main propulsion plant through pneumatic brakes. Simple mechanical or electrical switches usually control the mechanically operated actuating mechanism.

Propeller Problems

One of the major problems encountered with propellers is known as *cavitation*. Cavitation is the formation of a vacuum around a propeller, which is revolving at a speed above a certain critical value (which varies, depending upon the size, number, and shape of the propeller blades). The speed at which cavitation begins to occur is different in different types of ships; the turbulence increases in proportion to the propeller rpm. Specifically, a propeller rotating at a high speed will develop a stream velocity that creates a low-pressure. This low-pressure is less than the vaporization point of the water, and from each blade tip, there appears to develop a spiral of bubbles. The water boils at the low-pressure points. As the vapor bubbles of cavitation move into regions where the pressure is higher, the bubbles collapse rapidly and produce a high-pitched noise.

The net result of cavitation is to produce: (1) high level of underwater noise; (2) erosion of propeller blades; (3) vibration with subsequent blade failure from metallic fatigue; and (4) overall loss in propeller efficiency, requiring a proportionate increase in power for a given speed.

In naval warfare, the movements of surface ships and submarines can be plotted by sonar bearings on propeller noise. Because of the high static water pressure at submarine operational depths, cavitation sets in when a submarine is operating at a much higher rpm than when near the surface. For obvious reasons, a submarine that is under attack will immediately dive deep so that it can use high propeller rpm with the least amount of noise.

A certain amount of vibration is always present aboard ship. However, *propeller vibration* may also be caused by a fouled blade or by seaweed. If a propeller strikes a submerged object, the blades may be nicked.

Another propeller phenomenon is the *"singing" propeller.* The usual cause of this noise is that the trailing edges of the blades have not been properly prepared before installation. The flutter caused by the flow around the edges may induce a resonant vibration. A "singing" propeller can be heard for a great distance.

Bearings

From the standpoint of mechanics, the term *bearing* may be applied to anything that supports a moving element of a machine. However, this section is concerned only with those bearings that support or confine the motion of sliding, rotating, and oscillating parts on revolving shafts or movable surfaces of naval machinery.

In view of the fact that naval machinery is constantly exposed to varying operating conditions, bearing material must meet rigid standards. A number of nonferrous alloys are used as bearing metals. In general, these alloys are tin-base, lead-base, copper-base, or aluminum-base alloys. The term *babbitt metal* is often used for lead-base and tin-base alloys.

Bearings must be made of materials that will withstand varying pressures and yet permit the surfaces to move with minimum wear and friction. In addition, bearings must be held in position with very close tolerances permitting freedom of movement and quiet operation. In view of these requirements, good bearing materials must possess a combination of the following five characteristics for a given application:

1. The compressive strength of the bearing alloy at maximum operating temperature must be such as to withstand high loads without cracking or deforming.
2. Bearing alloys must have high fatigue resistance to prevent cracking and flaking under varying operating conditions.
3. Bearing alloys must have high thermal conductivity to prevent localized hot spots with resultant fatigue and seizure.
4. The bearing materials must be capable of retaining an effective oil film.
5. The bearing materials must be highly resistant to corrosion.

Classification

The reciprocating and rotating elements or members, supported by bearings, may be subject to external loads that can be resolved into components having normal, radial, or axial directions, or a combination of the two. Bearings are generally classified as sliding surface (friction) or rolling contact (antifriction) bearings.

Sliding surface bearings may be defined broadly as those bearings that have sliding contact between their surfaces. In these bearings, one body slides or moves on the surface of another and sliding friction is developed if the rubbing surfaces are not lubricated. Examples of sliding surface bearings are thrust bearings and journal bearings, such as the spring or line shaft bearings installed aboard ship.

Journal bearings are extensively used aboard ship. Journal bearings may be subdivided into different styles or types, the most common of which are solid bearings, half bearings, two-part or split bearings. A typical solid style journal bearing application is the piston bearing, more commonly called a *bushing.* An example of a solid bearing is a piston rod wristpin bushing such as found in compressors. Perhaps the most common application of the half bearing in marine equipment is the propeller shaft bearing. Since the load is exerted only in one direction, they obviously are less costly than a full bearing of any type. Split bearings are used more frequently than any other friction-type bearing. A good example is the turbine bearing. Split bearings can be made adjustable to compensate for wear.

Guide bearings, as the name implies, are used for guiding the longitudinal motion of a shaft or other part. Perhaps the best illustrations of guide bearings are the valve guides in an internal combustion engine.

Thrust bearings are used to limit the motion of, or support a shaft or other rotating part longitudinally. Thrust bearings sometimes are combined functionally with journal bearings.

Antifriction-type or *rolling contact bearings* are so-called because their design takes advantage of the fact that less energy is required to overcome rolling friction than is required to overcome sliding friction. These bearings may be defined broadly as bearings that have rolling contact between their surfaces. These bearings may be classified as roller bearings or ball bearings according to shape of the rolling elements. Both roller and ball bearings are made in different types, some being arranged to carry both radial and thrust loads. In these bearings, the balls or rollers generally are assembled between two rings or races, the contacting faces of which are shaped to fit the balls or rollers.

The basic difference between ball and roller bearings is that a ball at any given instant carries the load on two tiny spots diametrically opposite while a roller carries the load on two narrow lines. Theoretically, the area of the spot or line of contact is infinitesimal. Practically, the area of contact depends on how much the bearing material will distort under the applied load. Obviously, rolling contact bearings must be made of hard materials because if the distortion under load is appreciable the resulting friction will defeat the purpose of the bearings. Bearings with small, highly loaded contact areas must be lubricated carefully if they are to have the antifriction properties they are designed to provide. If improperly lubricated, the highly polished surfaces of the balls and rollers soon will crack, check, or pit, and failure of the complete bearing follows.

Both sliding surface and rolling contact bearings may be further classified by their function as follows: radial, thrust, and angular-contact (actually a combination of radial and thrust) bearings. Radial bearings, designed primarily to carry a load in a direction perpendicular to the axis of rotation, are used to limit motion in a radial direction. Thrust bearings can carry only axial loads; that is, a force parallel to the axis of rotation, tending to cause endwise motion of the shaft. Angular-contact bearings can support both radial and thrust loads.

The simplest forms of *radial bearings* are the integral and the insert types. The integral type is formed by surfacing a part of the machine frame with the bearing material, while the insert bearing is a plain bushing inserted into and held in place in the machine frame. The insert bearing may be either a solid or a split bushing, and may consist of the bearing material alone or be enclosed in a case or shell. In the integral bearing, there is no means of compensating for wear, and when the maximum allowable clearance is reached, the bearing must be resurfaced. The insert solid bushing bearing, like the integral type, has no means for adjustment due to wear, and must be replaced when maximum clearance is reached.

The pivoted shoe is a more complicated type of radial bearing. This bearing consists of a shell containing a series of pivoted pads or shoes, faced with bearing material.

The *plain pivot* or *single disk type thrust bearing* consists of the end of a journal extending into a cup-shaped housing, the bottom of which holds the single disk of bearing material.

The *multi-disk type thrust bearing* is similar to the plain pivot bearing except that several disks are placed between the end of the journal and the housing. Alternate disks of bronze and steel are generally used. The lower disk is fastened in the bearing housing and the upper one to the journal, while the intermediate disks are free.

The *multi-collar thrust bearing* consists of a journal with thrust collars integral with or fastened to the shaft; these collars fit into recesses in the bearing housing which are faced with bearing metal.

This type bearing is generally used on horizontal shafts carrying light thrust loads.

The *pivoted shoe thrust bearing* is similar to the pivoted shoe radial bearing except that it has a thrust collar fixed to the shaft, which runs against the pivoted shoes. This type bearing is generally suitable for both directions of rotation.

Angular loading is generally taken by using a radial bearing to restrain the radial load and some form of thrust bearing to handle the load. This may be accomplished by using two separate bearings or a combination of a radial and thrust (*radial thrust*). A typical example is the multi-collar bearing which has its recesses entirely surfaced with bearing material; the faces of the collars carry the thrust load and the cylindrical edge surfaces handle the radial load.

Main Reduction Gear and Propulsion Turbine Bearings

Reduction gear bearings of the babbitt-lined split type are rigidly mounted and dowelled into the bearing housings. These bearings are split in halves, but the split is not always in a horizontal plane. On many pinion and bull gear bearings, the pressure is against the cap and not always in a vertical direction. The bearing shells are so secured in the housing that the point of pressure on both ahead and astern operation is as nearly midway between the joint faces as practicable.

Turbine bearings are pressure lubricated by means of the same forced-feed system that lubricates the reduction gear bearings.

Main Thrust Bearings

The main thrust bearing, which is usually located in the reduction gear casing, serves to absorb the axial thrust transmitted through the shaft from the propeller.

Kingsbury or pivoted segmental shoe thrust bearings are commonly used for main thrust bearings. This type of bearing consists of pivoted segments or shoes (usually six) against which the thrust collar revolves. Ahead or astern axial motion of the shaft, to which the thrust collar is secured, is thereby restrained by the action of the thrust shoes against the thrust collar. These bearings operate on the principle that a wedge-shaped film of oil is more readily formed and maintained than a flat film and that it can therefore carry heavier loads for any given size.

In a segmental pivoted-shoe thrust bearing, upper leveling plates upon which the shoes rest and lower leveling plates equalize the thrust load among the shoes. The base ring, which supports the lower leveling plates, holds the plates in place and transmits the thrust on the plates to the ship's structure. Shoe supports (hardened steel buttons or pivots) located between the shoes and the upper leveling plates enable the shoe segments to assume the angle required to pivot the shoes against the upper leveling plates. Pins and dowels hold the upper and lower leveling plates in position, allowing ample play between the base ring and the plates to ensure freedom of movement of the leveling plates. The base ring is kept from turning by its notched construction, which secures the ring to its housing.

Main Line Shaft Bearings

Bearings which support the propulsion line shafting and which are located inside the hull kare called *line shaft bearings*, *spring bearings*, or *line bearings*. These bearings are of the ring-oiled, babbitt-faced, spherical-seated, shell type. The bearing is designed to align itself to support the weight of the shafting. The spring bearings of all modern naval ships are provided with both upper and lower self-aligning bearing halves.

Stern Tube and Strut Bearings

The stern tube is a steel tube built into the ship's structure for the purpose of supporting and enclosing the propulsion shafting where it pierces the hull of the ship. The section of the shafting enclosed and supported by the stern tube is called the *stern tube shaft*. The propeller shaft is supported at the stern by two bearings, one at each end of the stern tube. These bearings are called *stern tube bearings*. A packing gland known as the *stern tube gland* is located at the inner end of the stern tube. This gland, seals the area between the shaft and the stern tube, but still allows the shaft to rotate.

The stuffing box of the stern tube gland is flanged and bolted to the stern tube. The casting is divided into two annular compartments. The forward space is the stuffing box proper; the after space has a flushing connection for providing a positive flow of water through the stern tube for lubricating, cooling, and flushing. The flushing connection is supplied by the fire and flushing system. A drain connection may be provided.

A strut bearing has a composition bushing which is split longitudinally into two halves. The outer surface of the bushing is machined with steps to bear on matching landings in the bore of the strut. One end is bolted to the strut.

The shells of both stern tube and strut bearings are of bronze lined with a suitable bearing wearing material. The shells are normally grooved longitudinally to receive strips of laminated resin bonded composition or strips of composition faced with rubber or synthetic rubber compounds as wearing materials. The laminated strips are cut and installed in the bearing shell to present the end grain to the shaft. In naval craft other than major combatant ships, resin bonded composition bearings or full molded rubber faced bearings are used.

Propulsion Shafting

The propulsion shafting, which ranges in diameter from 18 to 21 inches for small twin-screw destroyers to approximately 30 inches for large four-screw carriers, is divided into four functional sections: the thrust shaft, the line shaft, the stern tube shaft, and the propeller or tail shaft.

Segments of the line shaft and the thrust shaft are joined together with integral flange-type couplings. The stern tube shaft is joined to the after end of the line shaft with an inboard stern tube coupling which has a removable after-sleeve flange. The tail shaft is joined to the stern tube shaft by a muff-type outboard coupling.

On single-screw ships, the portion of the out-board shaft which turns in the stern tube bearing is normally covered with a shrunk-on composition sleeve. This is done to protect the shaft from corrosion and to provide a suitable journal for the water-lubricated bearings. On multiple-screw ships, these sleeves normally cover only the bearing areas; on such ships, the exposed shafting between the sleeves is covered with synthetic sheet rubber to protect the shafting from seawater corrosion.

On carriers and cruisers, the wet shafting—that is, the shafting outboard in the sea— is composed of three sections: a tail shaft, an intermediate or dropout section, and a stern tube section. Integral flanged ends of these sections are usually used for joining the sections together.

Circular steel or composition shields known as *fairwaters* are secured to the bearing bushings of the stern tube and strut bearings and to both the forward and the after ends of the underwater outboard couplings. These are intended primarily to reduce underwater resistance. The coupling fairwaters are secured to both the shaft and coupling flanges and are filled with tallow to protect the coupling from corrosion.

Reduction Gears

Reduction gears are used in many propulsion plants to allow both the prime mover and the propeller to operate at the most efficient speed. Reduction gears are also used in many kinds of auxiliary machinery, where they serve the same purpose. There are various gear forms commonly used in shipboard machinery.

Reduction gears are classified by the number of steps used to bring about speed reduction and by the general arrangement of the gearing. A *single reduction gear* consists of a small pinion gear that is driven by the turbine shaft and a large main gear (or bull gear) which is driven by the pinion. In this type of arrangement, the ratio of speed reduction is proportional to the diameters of the pinion and the bull gear. In a 2 to 1 single reduction gear, for example, the diameter of the driven gear is twice that of the driving pinion. In a 10 to 1 single reduction gear, the diameter of the driven gear is ten times that of the pinion.

All main reduction gearing in current combatant ships makes use of double helical gears (sometimes referred to as *herringbone gears*).

Double helical gears have smoother action and less tooth shock than single reduction gears. Since the double helical gears have two sets of teeth at complementary angles, end thrust (such as is developed in single helical gears) is prevented.

In the double reduction gears used on most ships, a high-speed pinion that is connected to the turbine shaft by a flexible coupling drives an intermediate (first reduction) gear. A shaft to the low speed pinion, which in turn drives the bull (second reduction) gear mounted on the propeller shaft, connects the first reduction gear. If we suppose a 20 to 1 speed reduction is desired, this could be accomplished by having a ratio of 2 to 1 between the high-speed pinion and the first reduction gear and a ratio of 10 to 1 between the low speed pinion on the first reduction gear shaft and the second reduction gear on the propeller shaft.

In a typical double reduction gear installation for the DD 692 class destroyer (built during World War II), the cruising turbine was connected to the high-pressure turbine through a single reduction gear. The cruising turbine rotor carried with it a pinion that drove the cruising gear, coupled to the high-pressure turbine shaft. Three bearings, one at the forward end of the turbine and one on each side of the pinion in the cruising reduction gear case supported the cruising turbine rotor and pinion.

The high-pressure turbine and the low-pressure turbine are connected to the propeller shaft through a locked train double reduction gear. First reduction pinions are connected by flexible couplings to the turbines. Each of the first reduction pinions drives two first reduction gears. Attached to each of the first reduction gears by a quill shaft and flexible couplings is a second reduction pinion (low speed pinion). These four pinions drive the second reduction gear (bull gear) which is attached to the propeller shaft.

Locked train reduction gears have the advantage of being more compact than other types, for any given power rating. For this reason, all high-powered modern combatant ships have locked train reduction gears. Another type of reduction gearing, known as nested gearing, is used on most auxiliary ships but is not used on combatant ships. As may be seen, the nested gearing is relatively simple; it employs no quill shafts and uses a minimum number of bearings and flexible couplings.

Flexible Couplings

Propulsion turbine shafts are connected to the reduction gears by flexible couplings that are designed to take care of very slight misalignment between the two units. Most flexible couplings are of the gear type and consist of two shaft rings having internal gear teeth and an internal floating member (or distance piece) which has external teeth around the periphery at each end. The shaft rings are bolted to flanges on the two shafts to be connected; the floating member is placed so that its teeth engage with those of the shaft rings.

Cruising turbine couplings that transmit lower powers may use external floating members with internal teeth. With this design, the shaft rings become spur gears with external teeth on the ends of the pinion shaft and turbine shaft. The coupling is installed between the cruising turbine reduction gear and the high-pressure turbine. In this coupling, the floating member is a transversely split sleeve having internal teeth which mesh completely with the external teeth of the spur gears mounted on the connected shaft ends.

Care of Reduction Gears, Shafting and Bearings

The main reduction gear is one of the largest and most expensive units of machinery found in the engineering department. Main reduction gears that are installed properly and operated properly will give years of satisfactory service. However, a serious casualty to main reduction gears will either put the ship out of commission or force it to operate at reduced speed.

Extensive repairs to the main reduction gear can be very expensive because they usually have to be made at a shipyard.

Some things are essential for the proper operation of reduction gears. Proper lubrication includes supplying the required amount of oil to the gears and bearings, plus keeping the oil clean and at the proper temperature. Locking and unlocking the shaft must be done in accordance with the manufacturer's instructions. Abnormal noises and vibrations must be investigated and corrective action taken. Gears were inspected in accordance with the instructions issued by Naval Ships (NavShips), the type commander, or other proper authority. Preventive and corrective maintenance must be conducted in accordance with the 3-M System.

Proper Lubrication

Lubrication of reduction gears and bearings is of the utmost importance. The correct quantity and quality of lubricating oil must, at all times, be available in the main sump. The oil must be clean; and it must be supplied to the gears and bearings at the pressure and temperature specified by the manufacturer.

In order to accomplish proper lubrication of gears and bearings, several conditions must be met. The lube oil service pump must deliver the proper discharge pressure. All relief valves in the lube oil system must be set to function at their designed pressure. On most older ships, each bearing has a needle valve to control the amount of oil delivered to the bearing. On newer ships, an orifice in the supply line controls the quantity of oil to each bearing. The needle valve setting or the orifice opening must be in accordance with the manufacturer's instructions or the supply of oil will be affected. Too small a quantity of oil will cause the bearing to run hot. If too much oil is delivered to the bearing, the excessive pressure may cause the oil to leak at the oil seal rings. Too much oil may also cause a bearing to overheat.

Lube oil must reach the bearing at the proper temperature. If the oil is too cold, one of the effects is insufficient oil flow for cooling purposes. If the oil supply is too hot, some lubricating capacity is lost.

For most main reduction gears, the normal temperature of oil leaving the lube oil cooler should be between 120° F and 130° F. For full power operation, the temperature of the oil leaving the bearings should be between 140° F and 160° F. The maximum *temperature rise* of oil passing through any gear or bearing, under any operating conditions, should not exceed 50° F; and the final temperature of the oil leaving the gear or bearing should not exceed 180 °F. This temperature rise and limitation may be determined by installed thermometers or resistance temperature elements.

Cleanliness of lubricating oil cannot be overstressed. Oil must be free from impurities, such as water, grit, metal, and dirt. Particular care must be taken to clean out metal flakes and dirt when new gears are wearing in or when gears have been opened for inspection. Lint or dirt, if left in the system may clog the oil spray nozzles. The spray nozzles must be kept open at all times. Spray nozzles must never be altered without the authorization of the Naval Ship Systems Command.

The lube oil strainers perform satisfactorily under normal operating conditions, but they cannot trap particles of metal and dirt, which are fine enough to pass through the mesh. These fine particles can become embedded in the bearing metal and cause wear on the bearings and journals. These fine abrasive particles passing through the gear teeth act like a lapping compound and remove metal from the teeth.

Locking and unlocking the Main Shaft

In an emergency, or in the event of a casualty to the main propulsion machinery of a turbine-driven ship, it may be necessary to stop and lock a propeller shaft to prevent damage to the machinery. When the shaft is stopped, engaging the turning gear and then applying the brake is the most expeditious means of locking a propeller shaft while under way.

By carrying out actual drills, engine-room personnel should be trained to safely lock and unlock the main shaft. Each steaming watch should have sufficient trained personnel available to stop and lock the main shaft.

Caution: During drills, the shaft should not be locked more than 5 minutes, if possible. The ahead throttle should *never* be opened when the turning gear is engaged. The torque produced by the ahead engines is in the same direction as the torque of the locked shaft; to open the ahead throttle would result in damage to the turning gear.

The maximum safe operating speed of a ship with a locked shaft can be found in the manufacturer's technical manual. Additional information on the safe maximum speed that your ship can steam with a locked shaft can be found in Naval Ships' Technical Manual, Chapter 9410. If the shaft has been locked for 5 minutes or more, the turbine rotors may have become bowed, and special precautions are recommended. Before the shaft is allowed to turn, men should be stationed at the turbines to check for unusual noises and vibration. When the turning gear is disengaged, the astern throttle should be slowly closed; the torque produced by the propeller passing through the water will start the shaft rotating. If, when the propeller starts to turn, vibration indicates a bowed rotor, the ship's speed should be reduced to the point where little or no vibration of the turbine is noticeable and this speed should be maintained until the rotor is straightened. If operation at such a slow speed is not practicable, the turbines should be slowed by use of the astern throttle, to the point of least vibration but with the turbines still operating in the ahead direction. When the turbines are slowed to the point of little or no vibration, the shaft should be operated at that speed and the ahead throttle should be opened slightly to permit some steam flow through the affected turbine. The heat from the steam will warm the shaft and aid in straightening it. Lowering the main condenser vacuum will add additional heat to the turbines; this will increase the exhaust pressure and temperature.

As the vibration decreases, the astern throttle can be closed gradually, allowing the speed of the shaft to increase. The shaft speed should be increased slowly and a check for vibration should be maintained. The turbine is not ready for normal operation until vibration has disappeared at all possible speeds.

Noises and Vibration

On steam-turbine driven ships, noises may occur at low speeds or when maneuvering, or when passing through shallow water. Generally, these noises do not result from any defect in the propulsion machinery and will not occur during normal operation. A rumbling sound that occurs at low shaft rpm is generally due to the low-pressure turbine gearing floating through its backlash. This condition has also been experienced with cruising reduction gears. Vibrations initiated by the propeller cause the rumbling and thumping noises that may occur during maneuvering or during operation in shallow water. These noises referred to were characteristic only of some ships and were regarded as normal sounds for these units. These sounds disappeared with a change of propeller rpm or when the other causes mentioned were no longer present. These noises were usually being noticed in earlier destroyers when the ship was backing, especially in choppy seas or in ground swells.

A properly operating reduction gear has a definite sound that an experienced watchstander can easily learn to recognize. At different speeds and under various operating conditions, the operator should be familiar with the normal operating sound of the reduction gears on his ship.

If any abnormal sounds occur, an investigation should be made immediately. In making an investigation, much will depend on how the operator interprets the sound or noise.

The lube oil temperature and pressure may or may not help an operator determine the reasons for the abnormal sounds. A badly wiped bearing may be indicated by a rapid rise in oil temperature for the individual bearing. A certain sound or noise may indicate misalignment or improper meshing of the gears. If unusual sounds are caused by misalignment of gears or foreign matter passing through the gear teeth, the shaft should be stopped and a thorough investigation should be made before the gears are operated again.

For a wiped bearing, or any other bearing casualty that has caused a very high temperature, this procedure should be followed: If the temperature of the lube oil leaving any bearing has exceeded the permissible limits, slow or stop the unit and inspect the bearing for wear.

The bearing may be wiped only a small amount and the shaft may be operated at a reduced speed until the tactical situation allows sufficient time to inspect the bearing.

The most common causes of vibration in a main reduction gear installation are faulty alignment, bent shafting, damaged propellers, and improper balance.

A gradual increase in the vibration in a main reduction gear that has been operating satisfactorily for a long period can usually be traced to a cause outside of the reduction gears. The turbine rotors, rather than the gears, are more likely to be out of balance.

When reduction gears are built, the gears are carefully balanced (both statically and dynamically). A small amount of unbalance in the gears will cause unusual noise, vibration, and abnormal wear of bearings.

When the ship has been damaged, vibration of the main reduction gear installation may result from misalignment of the turbine, the main shafting, the main shaft bearings, or the main reduction gear foundation. When vibration occurs within the main reduction gears, damage to the propeller should be one of the first things to be considered. The vulnerable position of the propellers makes them more liable to damage than other parts of the plant. Bent or broken propeller blades will transmit vibration to the main reduction gears. Propellers can also become fouled with line or cable that will cause the gears to vibrate. No reduction gear vibration is too trivial to overlook. A complete investigation should be made, preferably by a shipyard.

Maintenance and Inspection

Under normal conditions, major repairs and major items of maintenance on main reduction gears should be accomplished by a shipyard. When a ship is deployed overseas and at other times when shipyard facilities are not available, a repair ship or an advanced base should accomplish emergency repairs, if possible. Inspections, checks, and minor repairs should be accomplished by ship's force.

Under normal conditions, the main reduction gear bearings and gears will operate for an indefinite period. If abnormal conditions occur, the shipyard will normally perform the repairs. Spares are carried aboard sufficient to replace 50 percent of the number of bearings installed in the main reduction gear. Usually each bearing is interchangeable for the starboard or port installation. The manufacturer's technical manual must be checked to determine interchangeability of gear bearings.

Special tools and equipment needed to lift main reduction gear covers, to handle the quill shaft when removing bearings from it, and to take required readings and measurements, are normally carried aboard. The special tools and equipment should always be aboard in case emergency repairs have to be made by repair ships or bases not required to carry these items.

The manufacturer's technical manual was the best source of information concerning repairs and maintenance of any specific reduction gear installation. Naval Ship's Technical Manual, Chapters 9420 (Propulsion Reduction Gears, Couplings, and Associated Components), 9430 (Shafting, Bearings, and Seals), and 9440 provided the inspection requirements for reduction gears, shafting, bearings, and propellers.

The inspections mentioned here are the minimum requirements only. Where defects are suspected or operating conditions so indicate, inspections should be made at intervals that are more frequent.

To open any inspection plates or other fittings of the main reduction gears, permission should first be obtained from the engineer officer. Before replacing an inspection plate, connection, or cover that permits access to the gear casing, a careful inspection shall be made by an officer of the engineering department to ensure that no foreign matter has entered or remains in the casing or oil lines. If the work is being done by a repair activity, an officer from the repair activity must also inspect the gear casing. An entry of the inspections and the name of the officer or officers must be made in the Engineering Log. The inspections required on the main engine reduction gears were located on the Maintenance Index Page.

The importance of proper gear tooth contact cannot be overemphasized. Any abnormal condition that may be revealed by operational sounds or by inspections should be corrected as soon as possible. Any abnormal condition, which is not corrected, will cause excessive wear that may result in general disintegration of the tooth surfaces.

If proper tooth contact is obtained when the gears are installed, little wear of teeth will occur. Excessive wear cannot take place without metallic contact. Proper clearances and adequate lubrication will prevent most gear tooth trouble.

If proper contact is obtained when the gears are installed, the initial wearing, which takes place under conditions of normal load and adequate lubrication, will smooth out rough and uneven places on the gear teeth. This initial wearing-in is referred to as *normal wear* or *running in*. As long as operating conditions remain normal, no further wear will occur.

Small shallow pits starting near the pitch line will frequently form during the initial stage of operation; this process is called *initial pitting*. Often the pits (about the size of a pinhead or even smaller) can be seen only under a magnifying glass. These pits are not detrimental and usually disappear in the course of normal wear.

Pitting which is progressive and continues at an increasing rate is known as *destructive pitting*. The pits are fairly large and are relatively deep. Destructive pitting is not likely to occur under proper operating conditions, but could be caused by excessive loading, too soft material, or improper lubrication. It is usually found that this type of pitting is due to misalignment or to improper lubrication.

The condition in which groups of scratches appear on the teeth (from the bottom to the top of the tooth) is termed abrasion, or scratching. It may be caused by inadequate lubrication, or by the presence of foreign matter in the lubricating oil. When abrasion or scratching is noted, the lubricating system and the gear spray fixtures should immediately be examined. If it is found that dirty oil is responsible, the system must be thoroughly cleaned and the whole charge of oil centrifuged.

The term "scoring" denotes a general roughening of the whole tooth surface. Scoring marks are deeper and more pronounced than scratching and they cover an area of the tooth, instead of occurring haphazardly, as in scratching or abrasion. Small areas of scoring may occur in the same position on all teeth. Scoring, with proper alignment and operation, usually results from inadequate lubrication, and is intensified by the use of dirty oil. If these conditions are not corrected, continued operation will result in a general disintegration of the tooth surfaces.

Under normal conditions all alignment inspections and checks, plus the necessary repairs, are accomplished by naval shipyards. Incorrect alignment will be indicated by abnormal vibration, unusual noise, and wear of the flexible couplings or main reduction gears. When misalignment is indicated, shipyard personnel should make a detailed inspection.

Two sets of readings are required to get an accurate check of the propulsion shafting. One set of readings is taken with the ship in drydock and another set of readings is taken with the ship waterborne—under normal loading conditions. The main shaft is disconnected, marked, and turned so that a set of readings can be taken in four different positions. Four readings are taken (top, bottom, and both sides). The alignment of the shaft can be determined by studying the different readings taken. The naval shipyard will decide whether corrections in alignment are necessary.

Note: During shipyard overhauls, the following inspections should be made:

a. Inspect condition and clearance of thrust shoes to ensure proper position of gears. Blow out thrusts with dry air after the inspection. Record the readings. Inspect the thrust collar, nut, and locking device.

b. If turbine-coupling inspection has indicated undue wear, check alignment between pinions and turbines.

c. Clean oil sump.

When conditions warrant or if trouble is suspected, a work request may be submitted to a naval shipyard to perform a "seven year" inspection of the main reduction gears. This inspection includes clearances and condition of bearings and journals; alignment checks and readings; and any other tests, inspections, or maintenance work that may be considered necessary.

Naval Ship Systems Command (currently Naval Sea Systems Command or NAVSEA) authorization is not necessary for lifting reduction gear covers. Covers should be lifted when trouble is suspected. An open gear case is a serious hazard to the main plant, therefore, careful consideration of the dangers of uncovering a gear case must be balanced against the reasons for suspecting internal trouble, before deciding to lift the gear case. The type commander may extend the seven-year interval if conditions indicate that a longer period between inspections is desirable.

The correction of any defects disclosed by regular tests and inspections, and the observance of the manufacturers' instructions, should ensure that the gears are ready for full power at all times.

In addition to inspections that may be directed by proper authority, the inspection plates were opened, and the examination of the tooth contact, the condition of teeth, and the operation of the spray nozzles were performed. It was not advisable to open gear cases, bearings, and thrusts immediately *before* full power trials.

After full power trials, the inspection plates were again opened, and an examination of the tooth contact and the condition of the teeth were performed to note changes that may have occurred during the full power trials. Running for a few hours at high power showed any possible condition of improper contact or abnormal wear that would not have shown up in months of operation at lower power. The clearance of the main thrust bearing was checked as well.

Safety Precautions

Personnel operating or working with propulsion equipment must observe the following precautions.

1. If there is churning or emulsification of oil and water in the gear case, the gear must be slowed down or stopped until the defect is remedied.
2. If the supply of oil to the gear fails, the gears should be stopped until the cause can be located and remedied.
3. When bearings have been overheated, gears should not be operated, except in extreme emergencies, until bearings have been examined and defects remedied.
4. If excessive flaking of metal from the gear teeth occurs, the gears should not be adjusted, except in an emergency, until the cause has been determined.
5. Unusual noises should be investigated at once, and the gears should be operated cautiously until the cause for the noise has been discovered and remedied.
6. The engineer officer should remove no inspection plate, connection, fitting, or cover that permits access to the gear casing without specific authorization.
7. The immediate vicinity of an inspection plate should be kept free from paint and dirt.
8. When gear cases are open, precautions should be taken to prevent the entry of foreign matter. The openings should never be left unattended unless satisfactory temporary closures have been installed.

9. Lifting devices should be inspected carefully before being used and should not be over- loaded.

10. When ships are anchored in localities where there are strong currents or tides, precautions should be taken to lock the main shaft.

11. Where the rotation of the propellers may result in injury to a diver over the side or in damage to the equipment, propeller shafts should be locked.

12. When a ship is being towed, the propellers should be locked, unless it is permissible and advantageous to allow the shafts to trail with the movement of the ship.

13. When a shaft is allowed to turn or trail, the lubrication system must be in operation. In addition, a careful watch should be kept on the temperature within the low-pressure turbine casing to see that windage temperatures cannot be built up to a dangerous degree. This can be controlled either by the speed of the ship or by maintaining vacuum in the main condenser.

14. The main propeller shaft must be brought to a complete stop before the clutch of the turning gear is engaged. (If the shaft is turning, considerable damage to the turning gear will result.)

15. When the turning gear is engaged, the brake must be set quickly and securely to prevent the shaft turning and damaging the turning gear.

16. When a main shaft is to be unlocked, precautions must be taken to disengage the jacking gear clutch before releasing the brake. If the brake is released first, the main shaft may begin to rotate and cause injury to the turning gear and to personnel.

17. In an emergency, where the ship is steaming at a high-speed, the main shaft can be stopped and held stationary by the astern turbine until the ship has slowed down to a speed at which the main shaft can be safely locked.

18. Where there is a limiting maximum safe speed at which a ship can steam with a locked propeller shaft, this speed should be known and should not be exceeded.

19. Before the turning gear is engaged and started, a check should be made to see that the turning gear is properly lubricated. Some ships have a valve in the oil supply line leading to the turning gear. The operator should see that a lube oil service pump is in operation and that the proper oil pressure is being supplied to the turning gear before the motor is started.
20. It should be definitely determined that the turning gear has been disengaged before the main engines are turned over.
21. While working on or inspecting open main reduction gears, the person or persons performing the work should not have any article about their person that may accidentally fall into the gear case.
22. Tools, lights, mirrors, etc. used for working on or inspecting gears, bearings, etc. should be lashed and secured to prevent accidental dropping into the gear case.

Steering

As noted at the beginning of this chapter, the direction of movement of a ship is controlled partly by steering devices that receive their power from steering engines and partially by the arrangement, speed, and direction of rotation of the ship's propellers.

The steering device is called a rudder. The *rudder* is a more or less rectangular metal blade (usually hollow on large ships) which is supported by a *rudder stock*. The rudder stock enters the ship through a *rudder post* and a watertight fitting. A *yoke* or *quadrant*, secured to the head of the rudder stock, transmits the motion imparted by the steering mechanism.

Basically, a ship's rudder is used to attain and maintain a desired heading. The force necessary to accomplish this is developed by dynamic pressure against the flat surface of the rudder. The magnitude of this force and the direction and degree to which it is applied produces the rudder effect, which controls stern movement, and thus controls the ship's heading.

In order to function most effectively, a rudder should be located aft of and quite close to the propeller. Many modern ships have twin rudders, each set directly behind a propeller to receive the full thrust of water. This arrangement tends to make a ship highly maneuverable.

Three types of rudders are in general use—the unbalanced rudder, the semi-balanced rudder, and the balanced rudder. Other types of rudders are also in naval use. For example, some ships have a triple-blade rudder that provides an increased effective rudder area.

CHAPTER 2

PROPULSION BOILER PLANTS

In the conventional steam turbine propulsion plant, the boiler was the source or high temperature region of the thermodynamic cycle. The steam that was generated in the boiler is led to the propulsion turbines, where its thermal energy is converted into mechanical energy that drives the ship and provides power for vital services.

In essence, a boiler is merely a container in which water can be boiled and steam generated. A teakettle on a stove is basically a boiler, although a rather inefficient one. In designing a boiler to produce a large amount of steam, it is obviously necessary to find some means of providing a larger heat transfer surface than is provided by a vessel shaped like a teakettle. In most modern boilers, the steam-generating surface consists of between one and two thousand tubes, which provide a maximum amount of heat transfer surface in a relatively small space. As a rule, the tubes communicate with a steam drum at the top of the boiler and with water drums and headers at the bottom of the boiler. The tubes and part of the drums are enclosed in an insulated casing that has space inside it for a furnace. As we will see presently, a boiler appears to be a fairly complicated piece of equipment when all its fittings, piping, and accessories are considered. Therefore, it may be helpful to remember that the basic components of a saturated-steam boiler are merely the tubes in which steam is generated, the drums and headers in which water is contained and steam is collected, and the furnace in which combustion takes place.

Practically all boilers used in the propulsion plants of naval ships from 1955 to 1990 were designed to produce both saturated steam and superheated steam. Consequently, to our basic boiler, we must now add another component: the superheater. The superheater on most boilers consisted of headers, usually located at the back or at the bottom of the boiler, and a number of superheater tubes that communicate with the headers. Saturated steam from the steam drum is led through the superheater; since the steam is now no longer in contact with the water from which it was generated; the steam becomes superheated without any appreciable increase in pressure as additional heat is supplied. In some boilers, there were separate superheater furnaces; in others, the superheater tubes projected into the same furnace that was used for the generation of saturated steam.

Some questions arose concerning the need for both saturated steam and superheated steam. Many steam-driven auxiliaries—particularly if they had reciprocating engines—required saturated steam for the lubrication of the moving parts of the driving machine. On the other hand, the propulsion turbines and many auxiliaries as well, performed much more efficiently when superheated steam was used. There was more available energy in superheated steam than in saturated steam at the same pressure, and the use of higher temperatures vastly increased the thermodynamic efficiency of the propulsion cycle since the efficiency of a heat engine depended on the absolute temperature at the source (boiler) and at the receiver (condenser). In some instances, the gain in efficiency resulting from the use of superheated steam may have been as much as 15 percent for 200 degrees of superheat. This increase in efficiency was particularly important for naval ships during past times because it allows substantial savings in fuel consumption and in space and weight requirements. A further advantage in using superheated steam for propulsion turbines was that it causes relatively little erosion or corrosion since it was free of moisture.

Boiler Definitions

In order to ensure accuracy and uniformity in the use of boiler terms, the Naval Ship Systems Command had established a number of standard definitions relating to boilers. Since these terms were widely used, the reader will find it helpful to understand the following terms and to use them correctly.

Boiler Full-Power Capacity. The total quantity of steam required to develop contract shaft horsepower of the ship, divided by the number of boilers installed in the ship, gives boiler full-power capacity. Boiler full-power capacity is expressed as the number of pounds of steam generated per hour at a specified pressure and temperature. Boiler full-power capacity is listed in the design data section of the manufacturer's technical manual for the boilers on each ship; it may be listed as capacity at full power or as designed rate of actual evaporation per boiler at full power.

Boiler Overload Capacity. Boiler overload capacity is usually 120 percent of boiler full-power capacity. Boiler overload capacity is listed in the design data section of the manufacturer's technical manual for the boilers; it may be listed as boiler overload capacity or as full power plus 20 percent.

Superheater Outlet Pressure. Superheater outlet pressure is the actual steam pressure carried at the superheater outlet.

Steam Drum Pressure. Steam drum pressure is the pressure actually carried in the boiler steam drum.

Operating Pressure. Operating pressure is the *constant* pressure at which the boiler is operated in service. Depending upon various factors, chiefly design features of the boiler, the constant pressure may be carried at the steam drum or at the superheater outlet. Operating pressure is specified in the design of the boiler and is given in the manufacturer's technical manual. Operating pressure is the same as superheater outlet pressure or steam drum pressure (depending upon which is used as the controlling pressure) *only* when the boiler is operating at full-power capacity, for combatant ships, or some other specified rate, for other ships. When the boiler is operating at less than full-power capacity (or other specified rate), the actual pressure at the steam drum or at the superheater outlet will vary from the designated operating pressure.

Design Pressure. Design pressure is the pressure specified by the boiler manufacturer as a criterion for boiler design. It is often approximately 103 percent of steam drum pressure. Operating personnel seldom have occasion to be concerned with design pressure; the term is noted here because there is a good deal of confusion between design pressure and operating pressure. The two terms do *not* mean the same thing.

Design Temperature. Design temperature is the intended

maximum operating temperature at the superheater outlet, at some specified rate of operation. The specified rate of operation is normally full-power capacity for combatant ships.

Operating Temperature. Operating temperature is the actual temperature at the superheater outlet. As a rule, operating temperature is the same as design temperature only when the boiler is operating at the rate specified in the definition of design temperature.

Boiler Efficiency. The efficiency of a boiler is the ratio of the Btu per pound of fuel absorbed by the water and steam to the Btu per pound of fuel fired. In other words, boiler efficiency is output divided by input, or heat utilized divided by heat available. Boiler efficiency is expressed as a percentage.

Fireroom Efficiency. Boiler Efficiency *corrected* for blower and pump steam consumption is called fireroom efficiency.

Note: Fireroom efficiency is *not* boiler plant efficiency or propulsion plant efficiency.

Steaming Hours. The term *steaming hours* is used to include all time during which the boiler has fires lighted for raising steam and all time during which steam is being generated. Time during which fires are not lighted is not included in steaming hours.

Total Heating Surfaces. The *total heating surface* of a boiler includes all parts of the boiler which are exposed on one side to the gases of combustion and on the other side to the water and steam being heated. The total heating surface equals the sum of the generating surface, the superheater surface, and the economizer surface. All heating surfaces are measured on the combustion gas side.

The *generating surface* is that part of the total heating surface in which water is being heated and steam is being generated. The generating surface includes the generating tubes, the water wall tubes, the water screen tubes, and any water floor tubes that are not covered by refractory material.

The *superheater surface* is that part of the total heating surface in which the steam is superheated after leaving the boiler steam drum.

The *economizer surface* is that portion of the total heating surface in which the feed water is heated before it enters the generating part of the boiler.

Desuperheaters. On boilers with non-controlled superheaters, all steam is superheated but a small amount is redirected through a desuperheater line. The *desuperheater* can be located in either the water drum or the steam drum; most generally, the desuperheater will be found in the steam drum below the normal water level. The purpose of the desuperheater is to lower the superheated steam temperature back to or close to saturated steam temperature for the proper steam lubrication of the auxiliary machinery. The desuperheater is most generally an "S" shaped tube bundle that is flanged to the superheater outlet on the inlet side and the auxiliary steam stop on the outlet side.

BOILER CLASSIFICATIONS

Although boilers vary considerably in details of design, most boilers may be classified and described in terms of a few basic features or characteristics. Some knowledge of these methods of classification provides a useful basis for understanding the design and construction of the various types of modern naval boilers.

Location of Fire and Water Spaces

One basic classification of boilers is made according to the relative location of the fire and water spaces. By this method of classification, all boilers may be divided into two classes: fire-tube boilers and water-tube boilers. In fire-tube boilers, the gases of combustion flow through the tubes and thereby heat the water that surrounds the tubes. In water-tube boilers, the water flows through the tubes and is heated by the gases of combustion that fill the furnace and heat the outside metal surfaces of the tubes.

All boilers used in the propulsion plants of modern naval ships are of the water-tube type. Fire-tube boilers (such as the Scotch marine boiler) were once used extensively in marine installations and are still used in the propulsion plants of some older merchant ships. However, fire-tube boilers are not suitable for use as propulsion boilers in modern naval ships because of their excessive weight and size, the excessive length of time required to raise steam, and their inability to meet demands for rapid changes in load. The only fire-tube boilers currently in naval use are some small auxiliary boilers.

Auxiliary boilers (some water-tube, some fire-tube) were installed in diesel-driven ships and in many steam-driven combatant ships. They are used to supply steam or hot water for galley, and other "hotel" services and for other auxiliary requirements in port.

Type of Circulation

Water-tube boilers are further classified according to the cause of water circulation. By this mode of classification, we have *natural circulation boilers* and *controlled circulation boilers*.

In natural circulation boilers, the circulation of water depends on the difference between the density of an ascending mixture of hot water and steam and a descending body of relatively cool and steam-free water. The difference in density occurs because the water expands as it is heated and thus becomes less dense. Another way to describe natural circulation is to say that it is caused by convection currents, which result from the uneven heating of the water contained in the boiler.

Natural circulation may be either free or accelerated. The generating tubes are installed at a slight angle of inclination, which allows the lighter hot water and steam to rise, and the cooler and heavier water to descend when the generating tubes are installed at a greater angle of inclination, the rate of water circulation is definitely increased. Therefore, boilers in which the tubes slope quite steeply from steam drum to water drum are said to have accelerated natural circulation.

Most modern naval boilers are designed for accelerated natural circulation. In such boilers, large tubes (3 or more inches in diameter) are installed between the steam drum and the water drums. These large tubes, called *downcomers*, are located outside the furnace and away from the heat of combustion, thereby serving as pathways for the downward flow of relatively cool water. When a sufficient number of downcomers are installed, all small tubes can be generating tubes, carrying steam and water upward, and all downward flow can be carried by the downcomers. The size and number of downcomers installed varies from one type of boiler to another, but some are installed on all modern naval boilers.

Controlled circulation boilers are, as their name implies, quite different in design from the boilers that utilize natural circulation.

Controlled circulation boilers depend upon pumps, rather than upon natural differences in density, for the circulation of water within the boiler. Because controlled circulation boilers are not limited by the requirement that hot water and steam must be allowed to flow upward while cooler water flows downward, a great variety of arrangements may be found in controlled circulation boilers.

Controlled circulation boilers have been used in a few naval ships during the late 1960s. However, in the 1970s, they were still considered more or less experimental for naval use.

Arrangement of Steam and Water Spaces

Natural circulation boilers are classified as drum-type boilers or as header-type boilers, depending upon the arrangement of the steam and water spaces. Drum-type boilers have one or more water drums (and usually one or more water headers as well). Header-type boilers have no water drum; instead, the tubes enter a great many water headers.

What is a header, and what is the difference between a header and a drum? The term header commonly used in engineering to describe any tube, chamber, drum, and similar piece to which a series of tubes or pipes are connected in such a way as to permit the flow of fluid from one tube (or group of tubes) to another. Essentially, a header is a type of manifold. As far as boilers are concerned, the only distinction between a drum and a header is the distinction of size. Drums are larger than headers, but both serve the same purpose.

Drum-type boilers are further classified according to the overall configuration of the boiler, with particular regard to the shape formed by the steam and water spaces. For example, double-furnace boilers are often called "M-type boilers" because the arrangement of tubes is roughly M-shaped. Single-furnace boilers are often called "D-type boilers" because the tubes form (roughly) the letter D.

An interesting variation in this terminology occurred when the single-furnace or D-type boiler became standard for steam-driven destroyer escorts and thus subsequently became known as a "DE-type boiler." The term "DE-type boiler" is still used rather freely; its use should be discouraged, however, as this general type of boiler is now installed on many ships other than destroyer escorts.

Number of Furnaces

All boilers that are now commonly used in the propulsion plants of naval ships may be classified as being either single-furnace boilers or double-furnace boilers. The D-type boiler is a single-furnace boiler; the M-type boiler is a double-furnace (or divided-furnace) boiler.

Furnace Pressure

Recent developments in naval boilers make it convenient to classify boilers based on the air pressure used in the furnace. Most boilers now in use in naval propulsion plants operate with a slight air pressure (seldom over 10 psig) in the boiler furnace. This slight pressure, which results from the use of forced draft blowers to supply combustion air to the boilers, is not sufficient to warrant calling these boilers "pressurized-furnace boilers." However, a new type of boiler has recently appeared on the scene and is being installed in some ships. This new boiler is truly a pressurized-furnace boiler, since the furnace is maintained under a positive air pressure of approximately 65 psia (about 50 psig) when the boiler is operating at full power. A special air compressor maintains the air pressure in the furnace. We must now make a distinction between this new pressurized furnace boiler, on the one hand, and all other naval propulsion boilers, on the other hand, with respect to the pressure maintained in the furnace.

Type of Superheater

On almost all boilers currently used in the propulsion plants of naval ships, the superheater tubes are protected from radiant heat by water screen tubes. The water screen tubes absorb the intense radiant heat of the furnace, and the superheater tubes are heated by convection currents rather than by radiation. Hence, the superheaters are referred to as convection-type superheaters.

On a few older ships, the superheater tubes are not screened by water screen tubes but are exposed directly to the radiant heat of the furnace. Superheaters of this kind are called radiant-type superheaters. Although radiant-type superheaters are not currently in use, it is not possible that they may come into use again in the future because of the lack of boiler designs.

Control of Superheat

A boiler that provides some means of controlling the degree of superheat independently of the rate of steam generation is said to have *controlled superheat*. A boiler in which such separate control is not possible is said to have *uncontrolled superheat*.

Until recently, the term *superheat control boiler* was used to identify a double-furnace boiler and the term *uncontrolled superheat boiler* (or *no control superheat boiler*) was used to identify a single-furnace boiler. Most double-furnace boilers now in use do, in fact, have controlled superheat, and most single-furnace boilers do not have controlled superheat. However, recent developments in boiler design make superheat control independent of the number of furnaces in the boiler. Single-furnace boilers *with* controlled superheat and double-furnace boilers *without* controlled superheat are both possible. The time has come, therefore, to stop relating the number of furnaces in a boiler to the control (or lack of control) of superheat.

Operating Pressure

For some purposes, it is convenient to classify boilers according to operating pressure. Most classifications of this type are approximate rather than exact. Header-type boilers and some older drum-type boilers are often called "400 psi boilers" even though the operating pressures may range from 300 psi (or even lower) to about 450 psi. The term "600-psi boiler" is often applied to various double-furnace and single-furnace boilers with operating pressures ranging from about 435 psi to about 700 psi.

The term "high-pressure boiler" is at present used rather loosely to identify any boiler that operates at substantially higher pressure than the so-called "600-psi boilers." In general, we will consider any boiler that operates at 751 psi or above as a high-pressure boiler. A good many boilers recently installed on naval ships operate at approximately 1,200 psi; for some purposes, it is convenient to group these boilers together and refer to them as "1200-psi boilers."

Classifying boilers by operating pressure is not very precise, since actual operating pressures may vary widely within one group. Also, any classification based on operating pressure may easily become obsolete. What was called a high-pressure boiler one day might well be called a low-pressure boiler the next.

BOILER COMPONENTS

Most propulsion boilers now used by the Navy have essentially the same components: steam and water drums, generating and circulating tubes, superheaters, economizers, fuel oil burners, furnaces, casings, supports, and a number of accessories and fittings required for boiler operation and control. The basic components of boilers are described here. In later sections of this chapter we will see how the components are arranged to form various common types of naval propulsion boilers.

Drums and Headers

Drum-type boilers are installed in the ship in such a way that the long axis of the boiler drums will run fore and aft rather than athwartships, so that the water will not surge from one end of the drum to the other as the ship rolls.

The *steam drum* is located at the top of the boiler. It is cylindrical in shape, except that on some boilers, it may be slightly flattened along its lower curved surface. The steam drum receives feed water and serves as a place for the accumulation of the saturated steam that is generated in the tubes. The tubes enter the steam drum below the normal water level of the drum. The steam and water mixture from the tubes goes through separators that separate the water from the steam.

Two sheets of steel are rolled or bent to the required semicircular shape and then welded together. The upper sheet is called the wrapper sheet; the lower sheet is called the tube sheet. Notice that the tube sheet is thicker than the wrapper sheet. The extra thickness is required in the tube sheet to ensure adequate strength of the tube sheet after the holes for the generating tubes have been drilled. The ends of the drum are enclosed with drumheads that are welded to the shell. One drumhead contains a manhole that permits access to the drum for inspection, cleaning, and repair.

The steam drum either contains or is connected to many of the important fittings and instruments required for the operation and control of the boiler.

Water drums and *headers* equalize the distribution of water to the generating tubes and provide a place for the accumulation of loose scale and other solid matter that may be present in the boiler water. In drum-type boilers, the water drums and water headers are at the bottom of the boiler. Water drums are usually round in cross section; headers may be round, oval, or square. Headers are provided with access openings. Water drums are usually made with manholes similar to the manholes in steam drums.

Generating and Circulating Tubes

Most of the tubes in a boiler are generating or circulating tubes. There are four main kinds of generating and circulating tubes: (1) generating tubes in the main generating tube bank; (2) water wall tubes, (3) water screen tubes, and (4) downcomers. The tubes are made of steel similar to the steel used for the drums and headers. Most tubes in the main generating bank are about 1 inch or 1 1/4 inches in outside diameter. Water wall tubes, water screen tubes, and the two or three rows of generating tubes next to the furnace are generally a little larger. Downcomers are larger still, being on the average about 3 to 11 inches in outside diameter.

Since the steam drum is at the top of the boiler and the water drums and headers are at the bottom, it is obvious that the generating and circulating tubes must be installed more or less vertically. Each tube enters the steam drum and the water drum (or water header) at right angles to the drum surfaces. This means that all tubes in any one row are curved in exactly the same way, but the curvature of different rows is not the same. Tubes are installed normal to the drum surfaces in order to allow the maximum number of tube holes to be drilled in the tube sheets with a minimum weakening of the drums. However, abnormal installation is permitted if certain advantages can be achieved in design characteristics.

What purpose do all these generating and circulating tubes serve? The generating tubes are the ones in which most of the saturated steam is generated. The water wall tubes serve primarily to protect the furnace refractories, thus allowing higher heat release rates than would be possible without this protection. However, the water wall tubes are also generating tubes at high firing rates. Water screen tubes protect the superheater from direct radiant heat. Water screen tubes, like water wall tubes, are generating tubes at high firing rates. Downcomers are installed between the inner and outer casings of the boiler to carry the downward flow of relatively cool water and thus maintain the boiler circulation. Downcomers are not designed to be generating tubes under any conditions.

In addition to the four main types of generating and circulating tubes just mentioned, there are a few large superheater support tubes, which, in addition to providing partial support for the steam drum and for the superheater, serve as downcomers at low firing rates and as generating tubes at high firing rates.

Since a modern boiler is likely to contain between 1,000 and 2,000 tubes, some system of tube identification is essential. Generating and circulating tubes are identified by *lettering* the rows of tubes and *numbering* the individual tubes in each row. A tube row runs from the front of the boiler to the rear of the boiler. The row of tubes next to the furnace is row A, the next is row B, the next is row C, and so forth. If there are more than 26 rows in a tube bank, the rows after Z are lettered AA, BB, CC, DD, EE, and so forth. Each tube in each row is then designated by a number, beginning with 1 at the front of the boiler and numbering back toward the rear.

An R or an L, particularly in the case of water screen tubes, superheater support tubes, and furnace division wall tubes, often precedes the letter that identifies a tube row. When an R or an L is used *after* the regular letter and number identification of a tube, it may indicate either that the tube is bent for a right-hand or left-hand boiler or that the tube is studded or finned on the right-hand side or on the left-hand side.

A letter does not identify the water wall tube row. The letter W and a following letter that indicates the type of tube or its position in the row often identify the tubes in this row. Still another letter (an R or an L) may be added to indicate that the tube is studded or finned on the right-hand side or on the left-hand side.

For example, the tubes, which screen the superheater from direct radiant heat, may be identified as the LA, LB, and LC rows. Within each row, the individual tubes are numbered: LA-1, LA-2, LA-3, and so forth.

The superheater tubes in this boiler, as in most boilers, are installed horizontally. The superheater support tubes and the drum support tubes are installed vertically; they are identified as LD-1, LD-2, LD-3, and so forth.

The first row of division wall tubes is identified as the LE row. The second row of division wall tubes may be identified as the LF row or as the D row. Identification of tubes in this row is usually made by using the row identification (LF, D, or whatever row identification is used for the particular boiler) followed by a letter to indicate the type of tube or its position in the row; still another letter (an R or an L) may be added to indicate that the tube is studded or finned on the right-hand side or on the left-hand side.

Tubes in the main generating bank are identified by lettering the rows and numbering the individual tubes. The two rows nearest the saturated-side furnace are slightly larger than the rest of the generating tubes; they serve as water screen tubes. These two rows are often called the RA and the RB rows. Number identifies individual tubes in these rows in the same way that the rest of the generating tubes are identified.

Note that the tubes is discussed in the section that deals with superheaters. The discussion of boiler tube identification given here is based on one particular type of boiler—that is, a double-furnace boiler. The same general principles of tube identification apply to most remaining drum-type boilers that may be in naval use, but the details of tube identification are necessarily different in different types of boilers.

Superheaters

Most propulsion boilers now in naval service have convection-type superheaters, with water screen tubes installed between the superheater and the furnace to absorb the intense radiant heat and thus protect the superheater.

Most convection-type superheaters have U-shaped tupes that are installed horizontally in the boiler and two headers that are installed more or less vertically at the rear of the boiler. One end of each

U-shaped tube enters one superheater header, and the other end enters the other header. The superheater headers are divided internally by one or more division plates, which act as baffles to direct the flow of steam. In some cases, the superheater headers are divided externally as well as internally.

There are different convection-type superheater arrangements that are used on double-furnace boilers. The steam makes several passes through the furnaces. The number of passes is determined by the number of header divisions and by the relative locations of the steam inlet and the steam outlet.

The superheater tubes are installed so that their U-shaped ends project forward toward the front of the boiler. In a double-furnace boiler, the superheater tubes project forward into a space between the water screen tubes and some tubes called *furnace division wall tubes*. The superheater tubes and the surrounding water screen and division wall tubes are thus together the dividing line between the superheater-side furnace and the saturated-side furnace. In a single-furnace boiler, the superheater tubes project forward into a space in the main bank of generating tubes. The tubes between the superheater tubes and the furnace serve as water screen tubes.

Some recent boilers have *walk-in* or *cavity-type* superheaters. In this type of superheater, an access space or cavity is provided in the middle of the superheater tube bank. The cavity, which runs the full length and height of the superheater, greatly increases the accessibility of the superheater for cleaning, maintenance, and repair. Some of the walk- in superheaters have U-shaped tubes. Others, have W-shaped tubes.

A few boilers of the 1960s design had vertical, rather than horizontal, convection-type superheaters. In these boilers, the U-bend superheater tubes are installed almost vertically, with the U-bends near the top of the boiler; the tubes are approximately parallel to the main bank of generating tubes and the water screen tubes. Two superheater headers are near the bottom of the boiler, running horizontally from the front of the boiler to the rear.

Generally, loop number, name of tube bank, and number of tube within the bank identify superheater tubes. In the case of horizontal superheater tubes, you count from the bottom toward the top to get the tube number. In the case of vertical superheater tubes, you count from the front of the boiler toward the rear.

Desuperheaters

On boilers with noncontrolled superheaters, all steam is superheated, but a small amount of steam is redirected through a desuperheater line, the desuperheater can be located in either the water drum or the steam drum, most generally, the desuperheater will be found in the steam drum below the normal water level. The purpose of the desuperheater is to lower the super-heated steam temperature back to or close to saturated steam temperature for the proper steam lubrication of the auxiliary machinery. The desuperheater is most generally an "S" shaped tube bundle that is flanged to the superheater outlet on the inlet side and the auxiliary steam stop on the outlet side.

Economizers

An economizer is installed on practically every boiler used in naval propulsion plants. The economizer is an arrangement of tubes installed in the uptake space from the furnace; thus the rising gases of combustion heat the economizer tubes. All feed water flows through the economizer tubes before entering the steam drum, and the feed water is warmed by heat, which would otherwise be wasted as combustion gases pass up the stack. In general, boilers operating at high-pressures and temperatures have larger economizer surfaces than boilers operating at low-pressure and temperatures.

Economizer tubes may be of various shapes. Most commonly, perhaps, they are a continuous loop of U-shaped elements from inlet to outlet header. Almost all economizer tubes have some sort of metal projections from the outer tube surface. These projections, which are of aluminum, steel, or other metal, are shaped in various ways. There are U-bend economizer tubes with aluminum gill rings that are circular in cross section. Other types of projections in use include rectangular fins and star-shaped disks. In all cases, the projections serve to extend the heat transfer surface of the economizer tubes on which they are installed.

Fuel Oil Burners

Almost all fuel oil burners used on naval propulsion boilers are mounted on the boiler front. Special openings called burner cone openings are provided in the furnace front for the burners.

The two main parts of a fuel oil burner are the atomizer assembly and the air register assembly. The atomizers divide the fuel oil into very fine particles; the air registers permit combustion air to enter the furnace in such a way that it mixes thoroughly with the finely divided oil. In addition to the atomizer assembly and the air register assembly, a fuel oil burner includes various valves, fittings, connections, and burner safety devices that prevent spillage of oil when an atomizer assembly is removed from the burner while the burner root valve is still open.

Atomizers

Three main kinds of atomizers are now in use on naval boilers. Straight-through-flow atomizers are used on most boilers. Return-flow atomizers were used on many of the newer ships from the 1970s, particularly those equipped with automatic combustion controls. Steam-assist atomizers were used on boilers in some of these newest 1970s ships.

There are fuel oil burners with a straight-through-flow atomizer. In a straight-through-flow atomizer, all oil pumped to the atomizer is burned in the boiler furnace. The fuel oil is forced through the atomizer barrel at a pressure between 125 and 300 psi. With this type of atomizer, the firing rate is controlled by changing the number of burners in use, the fuel oil pressure, and the size of the sprayer plates.

A straight-through-flow atomizer assembly consists of a gooseneck, a burner barrel (also called an atomizer barrel), a nozzle, a sprayer plate, and a tip. The fuel oil goes through the nozzle, which directs the oil to the grooves of the sprayer plate. These grooves are shaped so as to give the oil a high rotational velocity as it discharges into a small cylindrical whirling chamber in the center of the sprayer plate. The whirling chamber is coned out at the end and has an orifice at the apex of the cone. As the oil leaves the chamber by way of the orifice, it is broken up into very fine particles, which form a cone-shaped fog-like spray. A strong blast of air, which has been given a whirling motion in its passage through the burner register, catches the oil fog and mixes with it. The mixture of air and oil enters the furnace and combustion takes place.

The sprayer plates most commonly used are called standard sprayer plates. There are two types of standard sprayer plates: flat-faced or dished and rounded, and they may have four, six, or eight oil grooves. Standard sprayer plates with four grooves are most common.

Since the Department of Defense had authorized the conversion to a newer distillate fuel (NSDF), sprayer plates for burning this type of fuel were of the 6, 4, and 3 slot type. Sizes were also changed, as the viscosity of the new fuel was less than that of Navy special fuel oil (NSFO). Therefore, each class of ship needed the correct size sprayer plates to permit them to burn the correct amount of fuel for full power and overload conditions.

In a return-flow (also called a variable-capacity) atomizer, part of the oil supplied to the atomizer is burned in the boiler furnace and part is returned. Several types of return-flow atomizers are in use. One type (Todd) was designed to operate with a constant fuel oil supply pressure of 300 psig and a minimum return pressure of 25 psig. Another return-flow atomizer (Babcock & Wilcox) operates with a variable fuel oil supply pressure (up to 1,000 psi) and a variable return pressure, still another type (also Babcock & Wilcox) operated with a constant supply pressure of 1,000 psi and a variable return pressure.

The *return-flow* atomizer operates with a constant fuel oil supply pressure. The amount of oil burned in the furnace is controlled by regulating the oil return pressure. The supply oil enters through the tube-like opening down the middle of the atomizer barrel and passes through the sprayer plate. The tangential slots or grooves in the sprayer plate cause the oil to enter the whirling chamber with a rotary motion. As the oil reaches the return annulus, centrifugal force causes a certain amount of the oil to enter the return annulis. The amount of oil thus returned is determined by the backpressure in the return line; the backpressure is in turn determined by the extent to which the return line control valve is open. The oil that is not returned emerges from the orifice in the form of a hollow conical spray of atomized oil. The amount of oil burned is the difference between the amount of oil supplied and the amount returned.

The *straight-through-flow* atomizers and the return-flow atomizers just described are both considered to be mechanical atomizers of the pressure type. The steam-assist atomizer, now in use on some new ships, operates on different principles. The fuel oil enters a steam-assist atomizer at relatively low-pressure and is very finely atomized by a jet of steam. Combustion air is supplied by forced draft blowers, just as it is in other installations.

A *steam-assist* atomizer has two supply lines coming into it, one for fuel oil and one for steam. These two lines make the atomizer look a good deal like a return-flow atomizer. However, the steam-assist atomizer does not return any fuel oil; instead, all oil supplied to the atomizer is burned in the boiler furnace. Sprayer plates and other parts are somewhat differently shaped in steam-assist atomizers than they are in straight-through-flow atomizers and return-flow atomizers.

One reason why steam-assist atomizers have not been used for naval propulsion boilers until quite recently is that they use a considerable amount of steam that cannot be recovered and returned to the feed system. However, they have some advantages that tend to make up for this disadvantage. A major advantage is that the firing range of steam-assist atomizers is much greater than the firing range of other types of atomizers. This characteristic makes the steam-assist atomizer particularly useful for naval service, since it means that large changes of load can be made merely by varying the fuel oil supply pressure, without cutting burners in and out. The fuel oil supply pressure can be varied between 8 and 350 psi.

Air Registers

The main parts of an air register are (1) the movable air doors, (2) the diffuser, and (3) the stationary air foils. The movable air doors allow operating personnel to open and close the register. When the air doors are open, air rushes in and is given a whirling motion by the diffuser plate. The diffuser thus serves to make the air mix evenly with the oil, and to prevent flame being blown back from the atomizer. The stationary air foils guide the major quantity of air and cause it to mix with the larger oil spray beyond the diffuser.

Furnaces and Refractories

A boiler furnace is a space provided for the mixing of air and fuel and for the combustion of the fuel. A boiler furnace consists of a more or less rectangular steel casing that is lined on the floor, front wall, sidewalls, and rear wall with refractory material. The refractory lining serves to protect the furnace casing and to prevent loss of heat from the furnace. Refractories retain heat for a relatively long time and thus help to maintain the high furnace temperatures required for complete and efficient combustion of the fuel. Refractories were also used to form baffles, which direct the flow of combustion gases and protect drums, headers, and tubes from excessive heat.

There are many different kinds of refractory materials. The particular use of each type was determined by the chemical and physical characteristics of the material in relation to the required conditions of service. Refractories commonly used in the furnaces of naval propulsion boilers included firebrick, insulating brick, insulating block, plastic fireclay, plastic chrome ore, chrome castable refractory, high temperature castable refractory, air-setting mortar, and burner refractory tile.

Casings, Uptakes and Smokepipes

In boiler installations from 1955 through 1990, each boiler was enclosed in two steel casings. The inner casing was lined with refractory materials, and the enclosed space constituted the furnace. The outer casing extends around most of the inner casing, with an air space in between. Air from the forced draft blowers was forced into the space between the inner and the outer casings, and from there it flowed through the air registers and into the furnace.

The inner casing encloses most of the boiler up to the uptakes. The uptakes join the boiler to the smokepipe. As a rule, the uptakes from two or more boilers connect with one smokepipe.

Both the inner and the outer casings of boilers are made of steel panels. The panels may be flanged and bolted together, with gaskets being used at the joints to make an airtight seal, or they may be welded together. The casings are made in small sections so they can be removed for the inspection and repair of boiler parts.

Saddles and Supports

Each water drum and water header rests upon two saddles, one at the front of the drum or header and one at the rear. The upper flanges of the saddle are curved to fit the curvature of the drum or header, and are welded to the drum or header. The bottom flanges, which are flat, rest on huge beams built up from the ship's structure. The bottom flange of one saddle is bolted rigidly to its support. The bottom flange of the other saddle is also bolted to its support, but the bolt holes are elongated in a fore-and-aft direction. As the drum expands or contracts because of temperature changes, the saddle, which is not rigidly fastened to the support, accommodates to the changing length of the drum by sliding backward or forward over the support. The flanges which are not rigidly fastened are known as *boiler sliding feet.*

Airheaters

Some boilers of recent design have steam-coil airheaters to preheat the combustion air before it enters the furnace. A typical steam-coil airheater consists of two coil blocks, each coil block having three sections of heating coils in a single casing. Each individual section has rows of copper-nickel alloy tubes, helically wound with copper fins. Airheaters used in the past on some older naval ships were installed in the uptakes and the combustion gases preheated the combustion air; these airheaters thus utilized heat that would otherwise have been wasted. The use of these older airheaters was discontinued in naval ships because the saving of heat was not considered sufficient to justify the added space and weight requirements. The new steam-coil airheaters use auxiliary exhaust steam as the heating agent; they are installed near the point where the combustion air enters the double casing.

Fittings, Instruments and Controls

The major boiler components just described could not function without a number of fittings, instruments and control devices. These additional boiler parts are merely mentioned here for the sake of completeness.

Internal fittings installed in the steam drum may include equipment for distributing the incoming feed water, for separating and drying the steam, for giving surface blows to remove solid matter from the water, for directing the flow of steam and water within the steam drum, and for injecting chemicals for boiler water treatment. In addition, many boilers have desuperheaters for desuperheating the steam needed for auxiliary purposes.

External fittings and instruments used on naval boilers may include drains and vents; sampling connections, feed stop and check valves; steam stop valves; safety valves; soot blowers, watergage glasses and remote water level indicators; pressure and temperature gages; superheater temperature alarms; superheater steam flow indicators; smoke indicators; and various items used for the automatic control of combustion and water level.

TYPES OF PROPULSION BOILERS

Now that we have examined the basic components used in most naval propulsion boilers, let us put these components together, so to speak, to see how they are arranged to form the types of boilers now used in the propulsion plants of naval ships. The order of presentation is more or less historical, starting with the header-type boiler (which is probably the oldest boiler design still in service), going on to double-furnace boilers and to both older and newer types of single-furnace boilers, and ending with the recently installed pressurized-furnace boiler.

Header-Type Boilers

Sectional header boilers, commonly called header-type boilers, were installed in many auxiliary ships.

Header-type boilers normally operate at 450 to 465 psig and are designed for a maximum superheater outlet temperature of 740° to 750° F. In capacity, they range from about 25,000 to about 40,000 pounds of steam per hour.

Header-type boilers are sometimes referred to as cross-drum boilers because many of them were designed to be installed with the steam drum athwartships rather than fore and aft. However, some header-type boilers are not of the cross-drum type.

Header-type boilers are also referred to occasionally as side-fired boilers. This term is used to indicate the location of the burners with respect to the position of the steam drum. However, the term "side-fired" tends to be misleading because the surface of a boiler along which the burners are installed is generally regarded as the front of the boiler. In this discussion, we will take as the front of the boiler the surface along which the burners are installed. From this point of view, then, the steam drum is installed lengthwise along the top of the boiler front.

The header-type boiler gets its name from the header sections that are connected by the generating tubes. There may be 12, 14, or 16 of these header sections, depending upon the size of the boiler. Half of the header sections are installed under the steam drum, at the front of the boiler. The other half are installed at the rear of the boiler, at a somewhat higher level. The header sections are installed at a slight angle from the vertical, leaning somewhat toward the front of the boiler. The angle of inclination of the headers allows the straight generating tubes (which enter the headers normal to the header surfaces) to slope slightly upward from the front of the boiler toward the rear, thus allowing free natural circulation within the boiler.

The header sections installed under the steam drum at the front of the boiler are known as downtake headers. Each downtake header is connected to the steam drum by a short downtake nipple. The lower end of each downtake header is connected to the junction header (sometimes called the *mud drum*) by a short nipple.

The header sections installed at the rear of the boiler are known as uptake headers. Each uptake header is connected to the steam drum by a large circulator tube which enters the steam drum slightly above the normal water level.

The generating tubes in this type of boiler are straight rather than curved. The generating tubes connect the downtake headers at the front of the boiler with the uptake headers at the rear of the boiler.

The superheater consists of U-bend tubes, an upper superheater header, and a lower superheater header. The superheater tubes are installed at right angles to the generating tubes, between the main bank of generating tubes and the water screen tubes.

The steam drum of a header-type boiler usually has a manhole at each end. The steam drum contains the internal fittings, including a desuperheater.

The furnace of a header-type boiler has four vertical walls and a flat floor. The side walls are water cooled, being covered by water wall tubes which form a part of the circulation system of the boiler. There are two water wall downtake headers, one at each corner of the boiler front, installed vertically in the space between the inner and the outer casing. Two vertical water wall uptake headers are similarly installed at the two rear corners of the boiler. The water wall tubes are rolled into a downtake header at the front and an uptake header at the rear; they are arranged on the same slope as the generating tubes.

Water is supplied to the water wall downtake headers from the junction header. Steam and water rise through the water wall tubes to the uptake headers, and then through the riser tubes that connect the uptake headers to the steam drum.

An economizer is located behind the steam drum, in the way of the combustion gas exit. The boiler is completely enclosed in an insulated steel casing, and an outer casing is installed in such a way as to form an air chamber between the inner and outer casings. The air inlet is at the rear of the boiler; an air duct beneath the furnace floor connects the front air chamber and the rear air chamber. The double-cased air chambers at the sides of the boiler are connected directly to the cold air inlet so that an air pressure is maintained in these side chambers at all rates of operation. Removable casing panels are located at various points to permit access for cleaning, inspection, and repair.

In summary, the header-type boiler is considered one which, on the basis of the classification methods given earlier in this chapter, has the following characteristics: It is a water-tube boiler with natural circulation of the free (not accelerated) type. It has sectional headers instead of water drums, and so is called a "header-type" boiler instead of a drum-type boiler. It has only one furnace—but the term "single-furnace boiler" is never applied to header-type boilers, possibly because such identification has not been needed. It is not a pressurized-furnace boiler. It does not have controlled superheat. It operates at a pressure of 450 to 465 psig; however, header-type boilers are quite often referred to as "400-psi boilers."

Double-Furnace Boilers

Double-furnace boilers (also called M-type boilers) were installed on most older destroyers and on many other combatant ships. These boilers were designed to carry a steam drum pressure of approximately 615 psig and to generate saturated steam at approximately 490° F. The saturated steam for auxiliaries went directly from the steam drum to the auxiliary steam system; all other steam went through the superheater. Double-furnace boilers were designed in various sizes and capacities to suit different installations. They range in capacity from about 100,000 to about 250,000 pounds of steam per hour at full power.

One of the two furnaces in this boiler was used for generating saturated steam; the other was used for superheating the saturated steam. Because each of the two furnaces can be fired separately, allowing control of superheated steam temperature over a wide range of operating conditions, the double-furnace boiler has long been called a "superheat control boiler." However, the control of superheat is not necessarily related to the number of furnaces. Therefore, this boiler is referred to as a double-furnace boiler, rather than as a superheat control boiler, even though the boiler does in fact have controlled superheat.

Since each furnace has its own burners, the degree of superheat can be controlled by proportioning the amount of fuel burned in the superheater-side furnace to the amount burned in the saturated-side furnace. When burners are lighted only on the saturated side, saturated steam is generated; when burners are lighted on the superheater side as well as on the saturated side, the saturated steam flowing through the superheater becomes superheated. The degree of superheat depends primarily upon (1) the firing rate on the superheater side, and (2) the rate of steam flow through the superheater. However, the rate of steam flow through the superheater is basically dependent upon the firing rate on the saturated side. Therefore, we come back again to the idea that the degree of superheat depends primarily upon the ratio of the amount of oil burned in the superheater side to the amount burned in the saturated side.

The flow of combustion gases in the double-furnace boiler is partly controlled by gas baffles on one row of water screen tubes and on one row of division wall tubes. The gas baffles on the water screen tubes direct the combustion gases toward the superheater tubes and also deflect the combustion gases away from the steam drum and the water screen header. The baffles on the division wall tubes by the saturated-side furnace keep the saturated-side combustion gases from flowing toward the superheater tubes, thus protecting the superheater when the superheater side is not lighted off. In addition, the baffles on the division wall tubes deflect combustion gases from the superheater side up toward the top of the saturated side, allowing the gases to pass toward the uptake without disturbing the fires in the saturated-side furnace.

The double-furnace boiler has a steam drum, one water drum, one water screen header, and one water wall header. All these drums and headers run from the front of the boiler to the rear of the boiler. Most of the saturated steam is generated in the main bank of generating tubes on the uptake side of the boiler; most of these tubes are 1 inch in outside diameter, but a few rows of 2- inch tubes are installed on the side of the tube bank nearest the furnace. The evaporation rate is much higher in the 1-inch tubes than in the 2-inch tubes, since the ratio of heat-transfer surface to the volume of contained water is much greater in the smaller tubes. The larger tubes are used in the rows next to the furnace because it is necessary at this point to provide a flow of cooling water and steam sufficient to protect the smaller tubes from the intense radiant heat of the furnaces.

Double-furnace boilers have anywhere from 15 to 50 downcomers, which vary in size from about 3 inches in outside diameter to about 7 inches OD. The downcomers are installed between the inner and the outer casings.

The use of large-tube downcomers and small generating tubes results in extremely rapid circulation of water. Only a few seconds are required for the water to enter the steam drum as feed water, flow through the downcomers, circulate through the water drum or header, rise in the generating tubes, and return to the steam drum as a mixture of water and steam. Some notion of the extreme rapidity of circulation may be obtained from the fact that water in the downcomers may flow at velocities of from 3 to 7 feet per second.

The economizer on a double-furnace boiler is usually larger than the economizer on a header-type boiler. As a rule, the economizer on a double-furnace boiler has about 60 U-shaped economizer tubes.

Based on the classification methods given earlier in this chapter, we may consider the double-furnace boiler as one that has the following characteristics: It is a water-tube boiler with natural circulation of the accelerated type. It is a drum-type (rather than a header-type) boiler. It has tubes that are arranged roughly in the shape of the letter M—hence it is often called an M-type boiler. It has two furnaces—one for the saturated side and one for the superheater side. It has controlled superheat. It operates at a pressure of about 615 psig, and is often called a "600-psi boiler."

The most important advantage of the double-furnace boiler arises from the fact that the separate firing of the superheater side allows positive control of the degree of superheat. In the double-furnace boiler, it is theoretically possible to maintain the maximum designed temperature at the superheater outlet under widely varying conditions of load. In a single-furnace boiler, where one source of heat is used both for generating the steam and for super-heating it, the degree of superheat increases as the rate of steam generation increases; and hence the maximum designed temperature at the superheater outlet is normally reached only at full power.

Most double-furnace boilers are designed to carry a superheater outlet temperature of 850° F; this is about 100° F higher than the superheater outlet temperature in a comparable single-furnace boiler, given the same quality of materials for boilers, piping, and turbines. The reason why a higher superheater outlet temperature can be used in a double-furnace boiler than in a comparable single-furnace boiler is that allowance must be made, in the single-furnace boiler, for the maximum superheater temperatures that might occur under adverse conditions of load.

In spite of the advantages resulting from the control of superheat, double-furnace boilers are no longer being installed in naval combatant ships. Experience with these boilers has revealed certain disadvantages, which during this time appear to outweigh the advantages of controlled superheat. Some of the disadvantages are:

1. In practice, it is not possible to maintain maximum designed superheat at low steaming rates. Only the steam for the main turbines and the turbogenerators goes through the superheater; at low firing rates, therefore, the steam flow through the superheater is generally not sufficient to permit a high firing rate on the superheater side. Thus under some conditions the steam supplied to the propulsion turbines and to the turbo-generators may be saturated or only very slightly superheated. Consequently, the double-furnace boiler is actually less efficient than the single-furnace boiler at low firing rates.

2. The double-furnace boiler is more difficult to operate than the single-furnace boiler, and requires more personnel for its operation. Once there is any appreciable load on the boiler, the high air pressure in the double casings and in the furnace make it difficult and even dangerous to light burners on the superheater side. In order to avoid this difficulty, operating personnel would have to be able to predict the need for superheat and light off the burners on the superheater side before the air pressure had become so high. Obviously, such prediction is not always possible.

3. The double-furnace boiler is heavier, larger, and generally more complex than a single-furnace boiler of equal capacity.

Single-Furnace Boilers

The older single-furnace boilers that were installed on many World War II ships differ in several important respects from the newer single-furnace boilers that have been installed on ships built since World War II.

A single-furnace boiler of the older type produces about 60,000 pounds of steam per hour at full power. At full power the steam drum pressure is about 460 psig, the superheater outlet pressure is about 435 psig, and the superheater outlet temperature is about 750° F.

This boiler does not have controlled superheat. When the boiler is lighted off, both the generating tubes and the superheater tubes are heated. In order to protect the superheater tubes from overheating, all steam generated in the boiler must be led through the superheater. The saturated steam goes from the dry pipe in the steam drum to the superheater inlet; it goes through the superheater tubes, out the superheater outlet, and into the main steam line.

Auxiliary steam must go through the superheater (in order to provide a sufficient steam flow to protect the superheater) but must then be desuperheated. Desuperheating is accomplished by passing some of the superheated steam through a desuperheater, which is basically a coil of piping submerged in the water in the steam drum. Heat transfer takes place from the steam in the desuperheater to the water in the steam drum. The desuperheated steam which passes out of the desuperheater and into the auxiliary steam line is once again at (or very close to) saturation temperature.

So far, we have considered the flow of steam as it occurs after the boiler has been cut in on the steam line. However, what happens when a cold boiler is lighted off? How can the superheater tubes be protected from the heat of the furnace after fires are lighted but before sufficient steam has been generated to ensure a safe flow through the superheater?

Various methods are used to protect the superheater during this critical period immediately after lighting off. Very low firing rates are used, and the boiler is warmed up slowly until an adequate flow of steam has been established. Many—but not all—boilers of this type have connections through which protective steam can be supplied from another boiler on the same ship or from some outside source such as a naval shipyard or a tender. This steam comes in (under pressure) through the superheater protection steam valve. It enters the superheater inlet, passes through the superheater tubes, goes out the superheater outlet, passes through the desuperheater, and then goes into the auxiliary exhaust line by way of the superheater protection exhaust valve.

On single-furnace boilers that do not have a protective steam system for use during the lighting off period, even greater care must be taken to establish a steam flow through the superheater. In general, the steam flow is established by venting the superheater drains to the bilges while warming up the boiler very slowly.

Based on the classification methods given earlier in this chapter, we may consider this older single-furnace boiler as one that has the following characteristics: It is a water-tube boiler with natural circulation of the accelerated type. It is a drum-type (rather than a header-type) boiler. It has tubes that are arranged roughly in the shape of the letter D—hence it is often called a D-type boiler. It has only one furnace. It does not have controlled superheat. It was often classified as a "600-psi boiler," although it actually operated at about 435 psig.

As previously noted, the degree of superheat obtained in a single-furnace boiler of the type being considered is primarily dependent upon the firing rate. However, a number of design features and operational considerations also affect the temperature of the steam at the superheater outlet.

Design features that affect the degree of superheat include (1) the type of superheater installed—that is, whether heated by convection, by radiation, or by both; (2) the location of the superheater with respect to the burners; (3) the extent to which the superheater is protected by water screen tubes; (4) the area of superheater heat-transfer surface; (5) the number of passes made by the steam in going through the superheater; (6) the location of gas baffles; and (7) the volume and shape of the furnace.

Operational factors that affect the degree of superheat include (1) the rate of combustion; (2) the temperature of the feed water; (3) the amount of excess air passing through the furnace; (4) the amount of moisture contained in the steam entering the superheater; (5) the condition of the superheater tube surfaces; and (6) the condition of the water screen tube surfaces. Since these factors may affect the degree of superheat in ways that are not immediately apparent, let us examine them in more detail.

How does the rate of combustion affect the degree of superheat? To begin, imagine a simple relationship in which the degree of superheat goes up directly as the rate of combustion is increased.

Such a simple relationship does, in fact, exist—but only up to a certain point. Throughout most of the operating range of this boiler, the degree of superheat goes up quite steadily and regularly as the rate of combustion goes up. Near full power, however, the degree of superheat drops slightly even though the rate of combustion is still going up. Why does this happen? Primarily because the increased firing rate results in an increased generating rate, this in turn results in an increased steam flow through the superheater. The rate of heat absorption increases more rapidly than the rate of steam flow until the boiler is operating at very nearly full power; at this point, the rate of steam flow increases more rapidly than the rate of heat absorption. Therefore, the superheater outlet temperature drops slightly.

Suppose that the boiler is being fired at a constant rate and that the steam is being used at a constant rate. If we increase the temperature of the incoming feed water, what happens to the superheat? Does it increase, decrease, or remain the same? Surprisingly, the degree of superheat decreases if the feed temperature is increased, more saturated steam is generated from the burning of the same amount of fuel. The increased quantity of saturated steam causes an increase in the rate of flow through the superheater. Since there is no increase in the amount of heat available for transfer to the superheater, the degree of superheat drops slightly.

Under conditions of constant load and a constant rate of combustion, what happens to the superheat if the amount of excess air is increased? To see why an increase in excess air results in an increase in temperature at the superheater outlet, we must take it systematically:

1. An increase in excess air decreases the average temperature in the furnace.
2. With the furnace temperature lowered, there is less temperature difference between the gases of combustion and the water in the boiler tubes.
3. Because of the smaller temperature difference, the rate of heat transfer is reduced.
4. Because of the decreased rate of heat transfer, the evaporation rate is reduced.

5. The lower evaporation rate causes a reduction in the rate of steam flow through the superheater, with a consequent rise in the superheater outlet temperature.

The term "excess air" is used to indicate any quantity of combustion air in excess of that which is theoretically required for the complete combustion of the fuel. Some excess air is necessary for efficient combustion, but too much excess air is wasteful.

In addition to this series of events, another factor also tends to increase the superheater outlet temperature when the amount of excess air is increased. Large amounts of excess air tend to cause combustion to occur in the tube bank rather than in the furnace itself; as a result, the temperature in the area around the superheater tubes is higher than usual and the superheater outlet temperature is higher.

Any appreciable amount of moisture in the steam entering the superheater causes a very noticeable drop in superheat. This occurs because steam cannot be superheated as long as it is in contact with the water from which it is being generated. If moisture enters the superheater, therefore, a good deal of heat must be used to dry the steam before the temperature of the steam can rise.

The condition of the superheater tube surfaces has an important effect on superheater outlet temperature. If the tubes have soot on the outside or scale on the inside, heat transfer will be retarded and the degree of superheat will be decreased.

If the water screen tubes have soot on the outside or scale on the inside, heat transfer to the water in these tubes will be retarded. Therefore, there will be more heat available for transfer to the superheater as the gases of combustion flow through the tube bank. Consequently, the superheater outlet temperature will rise.

The single-furnace boiler is lighter and smaller, for any given output of steam, than the double-furnace boiler. Because the single-furnace boiler supplies superheated steam at low steaming rates, the overall plant efficiency is better with this type of boiler than with the double-furnace boiler. The single-furnace boiler has the further advantage of simplicity of operation and maintenance. Although the single-furnace boiler considered here does not have controlled superheat, this lack is less important than might have been supposed, since some of the theoretical advantages of controlled super-heat have not been entirely realized in practice.

The basic design of the single-furnace boiler has been used increasingly. Except for experimental boilers, no double-furnace boilers have been installed on 1970s combatant ships since World War II. The newer single-furnace boilers operate at approximately 600 psi or at approximately 1,200 psi. Operating temperature at the super-heater outlet was commonly 950° F for the 1200-psi boilers; this is 100° F higher than the operating temperature of most double-furnace boilers, and 200° F higher than the operating temperature of the older single-furnace boilers.

One of the most noticeable differences between the much older and the newer single-furnace boilers was the change in furnace design. Higher heat release rates were possible in the newer boilers. Although these newer single-furnace boilers were not the type referred to as "pressurized-furnace" boilers, they did often use a slightly higher combustion air pressure than the older single-furnace boilers. The use of higher air pressure caused an increase in the velocity of the combustion gases, and the increased velocity resulted in a higher rate of heat transfer to the generating tubes. Because of the increased heat release rates, a newer single-furnace boiler was likely to have a water-cooled roof and water-cooled rear walls as well as water-cooled side walls.

In design details and in general configuration, the newer single-furnace boilers varied somewhat among themselves. In a 1200-psi boiler of the type installed on some post World War II destroyers (except for the additional water-cooled surfaces); this boiler is very much like the older single-furnace boilers. In contrast, in a type of single-furnace boiler that had been installed on some 1970s ships, the superheater tubes were installed vertically, rather than horizontally, between generating tubes and water screen tubes. Additionally, there was a separate water screen header for the water screen tubes; this feature is unusual in single-furnace boilers, though standard for double-furnace boilers.

New Types of Propulsion Boilers

The field of boiler design is by no means static. Although one trend predominates—that of using higher pressures and temperatures—there are almost innumerable ways in which the higher pressures and temperatures can be achieved. New types of boilers were constantly being developed and tested, and existing boiler designs were subject to modification and improvement. The newer types of boilers discussed here did not by any means exhaust the field of new designs; indeed, it must be emphasized that a wide diversity of design was still possible in this field.

Top-fired Boilers

A new boiler design that was being used on some auxiliary ships was the top-fired boiler. In this boiler, the fuel oil burners are located at the top of the boiler and are fired downward. The top-fired boiler utilizes certain new construction techniques, including welded walls. The boiler is of the natural circulation type, with a completely water-cooled furnace. The only refractory material that is exposed to the gases of combustion is the refractory that is installed in corners and in a small area around the burners. The top-fired boiler has an in-line generating tube bank and a vertical superheater. It was expected that the top-fired boiler will be much cleaner and would require less maintenance than the older boilers of more conventional design.

Controlled Circulation Boilers

Controlled (or forced) circulation boilers had been used for some time in stationary power plants, in locomotives, and in some merchant ships. Only a few controlled circulation boilers had been installed in the propulsion plants of naval ships, and of this few the majority were subsequently removed and replaced by conventional single-furnace boilers with accelerated natural circulation. However, in theory, controlled circulation had some very marked advantages over natural circulation, and it was entirely possible that improved designs of controlled circulation boilers may have been developed for use in naval propulsion plants.

In natural circulation boilers, circulation occurs because the ascending mixture of water and steam is lighter (less dense) than the descending body of relatively cool and steam-free water. As boiler pressure increases, however, there is less difference between the density of steam and the density of water. At pressures over 1,000 psi, the density of steam differs so little from the density of water that natural circulation is harder to achieve than it is at lower pressures. At high-pressures, controlled circulation boilers have a distinct advantage because their circulation is controlled by pumps and is independent of differences in density. Because controlled circulation boilers can be designed without regard for differences in density, they can be arranged ip practically any way that is required for a particular type of installation. A greater flexibility of arrangement is possible and the boilers may be designed for compactness, savings in space and weight requirements, and maximum heat absorption.

There are two main kinds of controlled circulation boilers. One type is known as a *once-through* or *forced flow boiler*; the other type is usually called a *controlled circulation* or a *forced recirculation* boiler. In both types, external pumps are used to force the water through the boiler circuits; the essential difference between the two kinds lies in the amount of water supplied to the boiler.

In a once-through forced circulation boiler, all (or very nearly all) of the water pumped to the boiler is converted to steam the first time through, without any recirculation. This type of boiler has no steam drum, but has instead a small separating chamber. Water is pumped into the economizer circuit and from there to the generating circuit, the amount of flow being controlled so as to allow practically all of the water to "he converted into steam in the generating circuit. The very small amount of water that is not converted to steam in the generating circuit is separated from the steam in the separating chamber. The water is discharged from the separating chamber to the feed pump suction, if it is suitable for use; if it contains solid matter, it is discharged through the blow-down pipe. Meanwhile, the steam from the separating chamber flows on through the superheater circuit, where it is superheated before it enters the main steam line.

In the boiler circuits of a controlled circulation (or forced recirculation) boiler, more water is pumped through the circuits than is converted into steam. The excess water is taken from the steam drum and is pumped through the boiler circuits again by means of a circulating pump. This type of boiler has a conventional steam drum, which contains a feed pipe, steam separators and dryers, a desuperheater, and other fittings. The boiler has an economizer, three generating circuits, and a superheater. Circulating pumps, fitted as integral parts of the boiler, provide positive circulation to all steam generating surfaces.

Both types of controlled circulation boilers have far smaller water capacity than do natural circulation boilers, and therefore have much more rapid response to changes in load. For this reason, automatic controls are required on these boilers to ensure rapid and sensitive response to fuel and feed water requirements.

Pressurized-Furnace Boiler

A boiler recently developed for use in naval propulsion plants is variously known as a *pressurized-furnace boiler*, a *pressure-fired boiler*, a *supercharged boiler*, or a *supercharged steam generating system*.

A pressurized-furnace boiler is unlike other operational boiler types in general configuration. The pressurized furnace is cylindrical in shape, with the long axis of the cylinder running vertically. The boiler drum is mounted horizontally, some distance above the pressurized furnace. The drum is connected to the steam and water elements in the furnace by risers and downcomers, all of which are external to the casing. Some boilers of this type are side-fired. Others are top-fired; the burners are at the top of the pressurized furnace, firing downward into the furnace.

The burners, specially designed for the pressurized-furnace boiler, are quite unlike any we have thus far considered. The burners are designed to burn distillate fuel rather than Navy Special fuel oil. There are no air register doors. There are three burners per boiler, and each burner includes a special type of straight mechanical atomizer (not return-flow) which utilizes three sprayer plates at the same time. All three burners are operated simultaneously, and all three sprayer plates remain in place in each atomizer. The sprayer plates operate in sequence to meet changing conditions of load. The design of these burners allows an enormously wide range of operation without cutting burners in or out and without even changing sprayer plates.

The generating tubes run vertically inside the pressurized furnace. The superheater is an annular pancake arrangement inserted into the bottom of the pressure vessel. The superheater is designed to be removed without disturbing the main components of the boiler.

The air compressor that supplies the combustion air under pressure is driven by a gas turbine. The air compressor and the gas turbine together are referred to as the *supercharger*. Part of the energy needed for driving the gas turbine is obtained from the combustion gases leaving the boiler furnace. The combustion gases expand through the gas turbine, and some of the heat is converted into work. This is the same kind of energy transformation that occurs in a steam turbine; the difference is that hot combustion gases, rather than steam, carry the energy to the gas turbine. After the combustion gases leave the gas turbine, some of the remaining heat may be used to heat feed water as it flows through an economizer.

There are no forced draft blowers in pressurized-furnace boiler installations. The supercharger takes the place of the forced draft blowers, thus greatly increasing plant efficiency. The steam saved by the use of a supercharger instead of forced draft blowers may amount to as much as 8 or 10 percent of boiler capacity.

Altogether, a pressurized-furnace boiler is not much more than half the size and half the weight of a conventional boiler of equal steam capacity. A large part of this saving of space and weight occurs because the increased pressure on the combustion gas side causes a very great increase in the rate of heat transfer to the water in the tubes. Forced draft blowers for conventional boiler installations furnish air pressures ranging from to 10 psig. In a pressurized-furnace boiler, the air compressor supplies combustion air at pressures ranging from 30 to 90 psig.

A smaller generating surface is required to generate the same amount of steam. Another cause of space and weight saving is that the general design of the pressurized-furnace boiler eliminates the need for much of the refractory material that is required in other boilers. A pressurized-furnace boiler may require only about 2,000 pounds of refractory, as against the 21,000 pounds or more usually required in a conventional boiler of equal capacity.

Increased efficiency, a substantial saving in space and weight requirements, a substantial reduction in ship's force maintenance requirements, shorter boiler start-up time, and better maneuverability and control are the major advantages of the pressurized-furnace boiler. Although some operational and maintenance problems do exist with this boiler, it appears likely that most of them can eventually be solved by increased training of personnel, increased precision in the erection of the boilers, and perhaps continued refinements of design and construction.

Boiler Water Requirements

1960s and 1970s naval boilers could not be operated safely and efficiently without careful control of boiler water quality. If boiler water conditions were not precisely right, the high operating pressures and temperatures of these boilers will lead to rapid deterioration of the boiler metal, with the possibility of serious casualties to boiler pressure parts.

Although our ultimate concern was with the water actually in the boiler, we cannot consider boiler water alone. We must also consider the water in the rest of the system, since we are dealing with a closed cycle in which water is heated, steam is generated, steam is condensed, and water is returned to the boiler. Because the cycle is continuous and closed, the same water remains in the system except for the water that is lost by boiler blowdown and the very small amount of water that escapes, either as steam or as water, and is replaced by makeup feed.

There are two kinds of boiler blowdown: surface blowdown and bottom blowdown. Surface blowdown is used to remove foam and other light contaminants from the surface of the water in the steam drum. Bottom blowdown is used to remove sludge and other material that tends to settle in the lower parts of the boiler. Both surface blowdown and bottom blowdown may be used to remove a portion of the boiler water so that it can be replaced with purer makeup feed, thereby lowering the chloride content of the boiler water. Surface blows may be given while the boiler is steaming; bottom blows must not be given until sometime after the boiler has been secured.

Although we must remember the continuous or cyclical nature of the shipboard steam plant, we must also distinguish between the water at different points in the system. This distinction is necessary because different standards are prescribed for the water at different points. To identify the water at various points in the steam-water cycle, the following terms are used:

Distillate or *sea water distillate* is the fresh water that is discharged from the ship's distilling plants. This water is stored in fresh water or feed water tanks. All water in the steam - water cycle begins originally as distillate.

Makeup feed is distillate used as replacement for any water that is lost or removed from the closed steam-water cycle.

Condensate is the water that results from the condensation of steam in the main and auxiliary condensers. This water is called condensate until it reaches the deaerating feed tank.

Boiler feed or *feed water* is the water in the system between the deaerating feed tank and the boiler.

Deaerated feed water is feed water that has passed through deaerating feed tank and has had the dissolved or entrained oxygen removed from it.

Boiler water is the water actually contained within a boiler at any given moment.

Sea water, the source of practically all fresh water used aboard ship, contains about 35,000 parts per million (ppm) of sea salts. This is equivalent to roughly 70 pounds of sea salts per ton of water. When sea water is evaporated and the vapor is condensed in the distilling plant, the resulting distillate contains about 1.75 ppm of sea salts, or roughly 70 pounds per 20,000 tons. In other words, distillate is actually diluted sea water—sea water that is diluted to about 1/20,000 of its original concentration. It is not "pure water." In considering water problems and water treatment, it is essential to remember that the basic impurity of sea water distillate would make water treatment necessary even if no other impurities entered the water from other sources. The salts that are present in sea water—and, therefore, to a lesser extent in distillate—are mainly compounds of sodium, calcium, and magnesium.

Although *makeup feed* enters the tanks as distillate, the makeup feed usually contains a slightly higher proportion of impurities than the distillate. The difference is accounted for by slight seepage or other contamination of the water after it has remained in the tanks for some time.

Just as distillate is diluted sea water, so *steam condensate* is basically a diluted form of boiler water. The amount of solid matter carried over with the steam varies considerably, depending upon the design of the boiler, the condition of the boiler, the nature of the water treatment, the manner in which the boiler is operated, and other factors. In general, condensate contains from 1.7 to 3.5 ppm of solid matter, or roughly 70 pounds per 20,000 to 10,000 tons. Condensate may pick up additional contamination in various ways. Salt water leaks in the condenser increase the amount of sea salts present in the condensate. Oil leaks in the fuel oil heaters may contaminate the condensate. Corrosion products from steam and condensate lines may also be present in condensate. Under ideal conditions, condensate should be no more contaminated than sea water distillate; under many actual conditions, it is more contaminated.

The solid content of the water (*Boiler feed water*) in the system between the deaerating feed tank and the boiler is essentially the same as the solid content of the condensate. The main difference between condensate and deaerated boiler feed is that most of the dissolved gases are removed from the water in the deaerating feed tank.

Practically all of the impurities that are present in feed water, including those originally present in the sea water distillate and those that are picked up later, will eventually find their way to the boiler. As steam is generated and leaves the boiler, the concentration of impurities in the remaining *boiler water* becomes greater and greater. In other words, the boiler and the condenser together act as a sort of distilling plant, redistilling the water received from the ship's evaporators. In consequence, the *boiler water* would become more and more contaminated if steps were not taken to deal with the increasing contamination.

As an example, suppose that a boiler holds 10,000 pounds of water at steaming level, and suppose that steam is being generated at the rate of 50,000 pounds per hour. After an hour of operation there would be approximately five times as much solid matter in the boiler water as there was in the entering feed water. Now if we continued to steam this boiler for another 2,000 to 4,000 hours without using blowdown and without using any kind of boiler water treatment, the boiler water would contain just about the same concentration of sea salts as the original sea water from which the distillate was made. In addition, the boiler water would contain increasingly large quantities of corrosion products and other foreign matter picked up in the steam and condensate systems.

If we continued to steam the boiler with the water in this condition, the boiler would deteriorate rapidly. To prevent such deterioration, it is necessary to do the following things:

1. Maintain the incoming feed water at the highest possible level of purity and as free as possible of dissolved oxygen.
2. Use chemical treatment of the boiler water to counteract the effects of some of the impurities that are bound to be present.
3. Use blowdown at regular intervals to remove some of the more heavily contaminated water so that it may be replaced by purer feed water.

Although there are many sources of boiler water contamination, the contaminating materials tend to produce three main problems when they are concentrated or accumulated in the boiler water. Therefore, boiler water treatment is aimed at controlling the three problems of (1) waterside deposits, (2) waterside corrosion, and (3) carryover.

Waterside deposits interfere with heat transfer and thus cause overheating of the boiler metal. In the general manner in which a water-side deposit causes overheating of a boiler tube in a boiler operating at 600 psi, the temperature inside a generating tube may be approximately 500° F and the temperature of the outside of the tube may be approximately 100° F higher. The temperatures used in this example do not apply to all situations in which a boiler tube is overheated. The exact temperatures of the inside and outside of the tube would depend upon the operating pressure of the boiler, the location of the tube in the boiler, the nature of the deposit, and various other factors. Where a waterside deposit exists, however, the tube cannot transfer the heat as rapidly as it receives it. The inside of the tube has reached a temperature of 800 ° F at the point where the waterside deposit is thickest. The tube metal is overheated to such an extent that it becomes plastic and blows out into a bubble or blister under boiler pressure.

Waterside deposits that must be guarded against include sludge, oil, scale, corrosion deposits, and products formed as the result of chemical reactions of the tube metal.

The term *waterside corrosion* is used to include both localized pitting and general corrosion. Most waterside corrosion is electro-chemical in nature. There are always some slight variations (both chemical and physical) in the surface of any boiler metal. These small chemical and physical variations in the metal surface cause slight differences in electrical potential between one area of a tube and another area. Some areas are anodes (positive terminals) and others are cathodes (negative terminals). Iron from the boiler tube tends to go into solution more rapidly at the anode areas than at other points on the boiler tube. Electrolytic action cannot be completely prevented in any boiler, but it can be kept to a minimum by maintaining the boiler water at the proper alkalinity and by keeping the dissolved oxygen content of the boiler water as low as possible.

The presence of dissolved oxygen in the boiler water contributes greatly to the type of corrosion in which electrolytic action makes pits or holes. A pit of this type actually indicates an anodic area in which iron from the boiler tube has gone into solution in the boiler water.

General corrosion occurs when conditions favor the formation of many small anodes and n the surface of the boiler metal. As corrosion proceeds, the anodes and cathodes constantly change location. Therefore, there is a general loss of metal over the entire surface. General corrosion may occur if the chloride content of the boiler water is too high or if the alkalinity is either too low or too high.

The third major problem that results from boiler water

contamination is *carryover*. Under some circumstances, very small particles of moisture (almost like a fine mist) are carried over with the steam. Under other circumstances, large gulps or slugs of water are carried over. The term *priming* is generally used to describe the carryover of large quantities of water. Both kinds of carryover are dangerous and both can cause severe damage to superheaters, steam lines, turbines, and valves. Whatever moisture or water is carried over with the steam brings with it the solid matter that is dissolved or suspended in the water. This solid matter tends to be deposited on turbine blades and in super-heater tubes and valves. In a superheater tube in which solid matter has been deposited as a result of carryover, priming, or the carryover of large slugs of water, is particularly dangerous because it can do such severe damage to machinery. For example, priming can actually rip turbine blades from their wheels. One cause of carryover is foaming of the boiler water. Foaming occurs when the water contains too much dissolved or suspended solid matter. The solids tend to stabilize the bubbles and cause them to pile up instead of bursting. If a great deal of solid matter is present in the boiler water, a considerable amount of foam will pile up. Under these conditions, carryover is almost sure to occur.

In order to counteract the effects of the impurities in boiler water, it is necessary to have a precise knowledge of the actual condition of the water. This knowledge is obtained by frequent tests of the boiler water and of the feed water. Boiler water tests include chloride tests, hardness tests, alkalinity tests, pH tests, phosphate tests, and electrical conductivity tests that indicate the dissolved solid content of the boiler water. No one ship makes all of these tests of boiler water. The types of boiler water tests required on any particular ship depend upon the method of boiler water treatment authorized for that ship. Feed water is tested routinely for chloride, hardness, and dissolved oxygen; alkalinity, pH, phosphate, and electrical conductivity tests are not normally made on feed water. The Naval Ship Systems Command specifies the frequency of boiler water and feed water tests and the allowable limits of contamination. In general, the requirements for purity of boiler water become more stringent with increasing boiler pressure.

Water tests aboard ship are made by the oil and water king (usually a Boiler Technician), although certain aspects of the preparation and handling of the chemicals may require the supervision of an officer. The tests require some knowledge of chemistry and a high degree of precision in preparing, using, and measuring the chemicals. Therefore, only personnel holding a current certification resulting from successful completion of a NavShips boiler water/feed water test and treatment training course was allowed test and treat boiler water and feed water on propulsion boilers.

Some of the water tests made aboard ship gave a direct indication of just what contaminating substance was present, and in just what amount it was present. In other cases, it is more important to know what effects the contaminating substances have upon the water than it is to know what the substances are or exactly how much of each is present. Therefore, some water tests were designed to measure properties the water acquires because of the presence of various impurities.

The term *chloride content* really refers to the concentration of the chloride ion, rather than to the concentration of any one sea salt.

Because the concentration of chloride ions is relatively constant in sea water, the chloride content is used as a measure of the amount of solid matter that is derived through sea water contamination. The results of the chloride test are used as one indication of the need for blow-down. Chloride content is expressed in equivalents per million (epm). Equivalents per million can be defined as the number of equivalent parts of a substance per million parts of some other substance. The word "equivalent" here refers to the chemical equivalent weight of a substance. For example, if a substance has a chemical equivalent weight of 35.5, a solution containing 35.5 parts per million is described as having a concentration of 1 epm.

Hardness is a property that water acquires because of the presence of certain dissolved salts. Water in which soap does not readily form a lather is said to be hard.

Alkalinity is a property that the water acquires because of the presence of certain impurities. On ships that make alkalinity tests, the results are expressed in epm.

Some ships are required to determine the pH value, rather than the alkalinity, of the boiler water. The pH unit does not measure alkalinity directly; however, it is related to alkalinity in such a way that a pH number gives an indication of the acidity or alkalinity of the water. The pH scale of numbers runs from to 14. On this scale, pH 7 is the neutral point. Solutions having pH values above 7 are defined as alkaline solutions. Solutions having pH values below 7 are defined as acid solutions.

Boiler water that was treated with phosphates had to be tested for *phosphate content*. Boiler water that was treated with standard Navy boiler compound was not tested for phosphates. Phosphate content is expressed in parts per million (ppm). When the phosphate content of boiler water is maintained within the specified limits, the hardness of the water should be zero. Therefore, hardness tests were not required for boiler water when phosphate water treatment was used.

The test for *chloride content* indicates something about the amount of solid matter that is present in the boiler water, but it indicates only the solid matter that is there because of sea water contamination. It does not indicate anything about other solid matter that may be dissolved in the boiler water. A more accurate indication of the total amount of dissolved solids can be obtained by measuring the *electrical conductivity* of the boiler water, since this is related to the *total dissolved solid content*. All ships are now furnished with special electrical conductivity meters for measuring the conductivity of the boiler water. The total dissolved solid content is expressed in micromhos, a unit of electrical conductivity.

Routinely, the test for *dissolved oxygen* was made only on feed water, although occasional testing of water in other parts of the system was recommended. A chemical test for dissolved oxygen is made aboard ship. Since this test cannot detect dissolved oxygen in concentrations of less than 0.02 ppm, more sensitive laboratory tests are sometimes made as a check on the operation of the deaerating feed tanks.

When tests of the boiler water show that the water is not within the prescribed limits, chemical treatment and blowdown are instituted. Several methods of chemical treatment are now authorized. Each method is designed to completely eliminate hardness and to maintain the alkalinity (or the pH value) within the prescribed limits. The method of boiler water treatment specified for each ship is the method that will best perform these two functions and, at the same time, take account of the total concentration of solids that can be tolerated in the particular type of boiler. The Naval Ship Systems Command specifies the type of water treatment authorized for any particular ship; it is not a matter of choice by ship's personnel.

Chemical treatment of the boiler water increases, rather than decreases, the need for blowdown. The chemical treatment counteracts the effects of many of the impurities in the boiler water, but at the same time, it increases the total amount of solid matter in the boiler water and increases the need for blowdown. Each steam boiler had to be given a surface blow at least once a day, and more often if the water tests indicate the need. Bottom blows were given at least once a week, usually about an hour after the boiler has been secured. Bottom blows was not given while a boiler was steaming. Special instructions for boiler blowdown were issued to certain categories of ships.

Combination Requirements

Certain requirements had to be met before combustion can occur in the boiler furnace. The fuel must be heated to the temperature that will give it the proper viscosity for atomization. It should be *noted*, however, that with the conversion to the new distillate fuel (NSDF), the fuel will not need to be heated as the viscosity is much lower than the fuel oil (NSFO) now being used. The fuel must be forced into the furnace under pressure through the atomizers which divide the fuel into very fine particles. Meanwhile, combustion air must be forced into the furnace and admitted in such a way that the air will mix thoroughly with the finely divided fuel. Finally, it is necessary to supply enough heat so that the fuel would ignite and continue to burn.

Combustion is a chemical process which results in the rapid release of energy in the form of heat and light. When a fuel burns, the chemical reactions between the combustible elements in the fuel and the oxygen in the air result in new compounds. The combustible components of fuel are mainly carbon and hydrogen, which are present largely in the form of hydrocarbons. Sulfur, oxygen, nitrogen, and a small amount of moisture are also present in fuel.

In almost all burning processes, the principal reactions are the combination of the carbon and the hydrogen in the fuel with the oxygen in the air to form carbon dioxide and a relatively small amount of water vapor. In the absence of sufficient air to form carbon dioxide, carbon monoxide will be formed. A reaction of lesser importance is the combination of sulfur and oxygen to form sulfur dioxide.

Atmospheric air is the source of oxygen for the combustion reactions occurring in a boiler furnace. Air is a mixture of oxygen, nitrogen, and small amounts of carbon dioxide, water vapor, and inert gases. The approximate composition of air, by weight and by volume, is as follows:

Element	Weight (Percent)	Volume (Percent)
Oxygen	23.15	20.91
Nitrogen, etc.	76.85	79.09

At the proper temperature, the oxygen in the air combines chemically with the combustible substances in the fuel. The nitrogen, which is 76.85 percent by weight of all air entering the furnace, serves no useful purpose in combustion but is rather a direct source of heat loss, since it absorbs heat in passing through the furnace and carries off a considerable amount of heat as it goes out the stack.

When a combustion reaction occurs, a definite amount of heat is liberated. The total amount of heat released by the combustion of a fuel is the sum of the heat released by each element in the fuel. The amount of heat liberated in the burning of each of the principal elements in fuel oil is as follows:

Element	Chemical Symbol	Heat Released by Combustion (BTU per lb)
Hydrogen (to water)	H_2	62,000
Carbon (to carbon monoxide)	C	4,440
Carbon (to carbon dioxide)	C	14,540
Sulfur (to sulfur dioxide)	S	4,050

Notice that much more heat is liberated when carbon is burned to carbon dioxide than when it is burned to carbon monoxide, the difference being 10,100 BTU per pound. In burning to carbon monoxide, the carbon is not completely oxidized; in burning to carbon dioxide, the carbon combines with all the oxygen possible, and thus oxidation is complete.

Up to this point in this discussion, we have assumed that the oxygen necessary for combustion was present in the exact amount required for the complete combustion of all the combustible elements in the fuel. However, it is not a simple matter to introduce just exactly the required amount of oxygen—no more, no less—into the boiler furnace.

Since atmospheric air is the source of oxygen for the combustion process that occurs in the boiler furnace, let us first calculate the amount of air that would be needed to furnish 1 pound of oxygen. By weight, the composition of air is 23.15 percent oxygen and 76.85 percent nitrogen (disregarding the very small quantities of other gases present in air). To supply 1 pound of oxygen for combustion, therefore, it is necessary to supply 1/0.2315 or 4.32 pounds of air.

Since nitrogen constitutes 76.85 percent of the air (by weight), the amount of nitrogen in this 4.32 pounds of air will be 0.7685 x 4.32 or 3.32 pounds. As mentioned before, the nitrogen serves no useful purpose in combustion and is a direct source of heat loss.

Calculations will show that approximately 14 pounds of air will furnish the oxygen theoretically required for the complete combustion of 1 pound of fuel. In actual practice, of course, the amount of air necessary to ensure complete combustion must be somewhat in excess of that theoretically required. About 10 to 15 percent excess air is usually sufficient to ensure proper combustion. Too much excess air serves no useful purpose, but merely absorbs and carries off heat.

When fuel is burned in the boiler furnace, the difference between the *heat input* and the *heat absorbed* represents the *heat loss*. Heat losses may be unavoidable, avoidable; or in some cases, avoidable only to a limited extent. Most heat losses may be accounted for, but some losses cannot normally be accounted for.

All fuel contains a small amount of moisture that must be evaporated and superheated to the furnace temperature. Since the expenditure of heat for this purpose constitutes a heat loss in terms of boiler efficiency, every precaution should be taken to prevent contamination of the fuel oil with water.

All fuel contains some hydrogen, which, when combined with oxygen by the process of combustion, forms water vapor. This water vapor must be evaporated and superheated, and in both processes, it absorbs heat. Consequently, although the heat of combustion of hydrogen is very great, a small heat loss occurs because the water vapor formed as a result of the combustion of hydrogen must be evaporated and superheated.

Since atmospheric air is the source of the oxygen utilized for combustion in the boiler furnace, there is bound to be some moisture in the combustion air. This moisture must be evaporated and superheated, and therefore constitutes a heat loss.

The heat loss due to heat being carried away by combustion gases is the greatest of all the heat losses that occur in a boiler. Although much of this heat loss is unavoidable, some may be prevented by keeping all heat-transfer surfaces clean and by using no more excess air than is actually required for combustion.

Another heat loss occurs because of incomplete combustion of the fuel. When the carbon in the fuel is burned to carbon monoxide, instead of carbon dioxide, there is a tremendous heat loss of 10,100 BTU per pound. This should be considered an avoidable loss, since the admission of a sufficient amount of excess air will ensure complete combustion.

Heat losses that cannot be measured or that are impracticable to measure are (1) losses due to unburned hydrocarbons, gaseous or solid; (2) losses due to radiation; and (3) other losses not normally accounted for.

Fireroom Operations

Although a complete discussion of fireroom operations is beyond the scope of this text, some understanding of the major factors involved in boiler operation may be useful.

Basically, the fireroom force must control three inputs—feed water, fuel, and combustion air—in order to provide one output, steam. Under steady steaming conditions, when steam demands are relatively constant for long periods, there was no great difficulty about providing a uniform flow of steam to the propulsion turbines. However, one of the special requirements of naval ships was that they had to be able to maneuver and to change speed quickly, and this requirement imposes upon the fireroom force the responsibility for making very rapid increases and decreases in the amount of steam furnished to the engine-room. Under conditions of rapid change, boiler operation was a teamwork job that required great skill and alertness and smooth coordination of efforts by several men.

For manual operation of the boilers, a normal fireroom watch consisted of one petty officer in charge of the watch; one checkman for each operating boiler; one burnerman for each operating boiler front; one blowerman for each operating boiler; and one or more men to act as messengers and to check the operation of the auxiliary machinery. When automatic boiler controls were installed, boilers were operated with fewer men on watch when the controls were being used.

When a boiler was being operated manually, the checkman controlled the water level in the boiler by manual operation of the feed stop and check valves. The checkman was positioned at the upper level, near the feed stop and check valves, and near the boiler gage glass. The checkman admits water to the boiler as necessary to maintain the water at or very near the designed water level. The check watch required the utmost vigilance and reliability; if any one job in the fireroom can be said to be more important than any other, the checkman's job was the one.

One of the greatest difficulties in maintaining the water level arises from the fact that the boiler water swells and shrinks as the firing rate is changed. As the firing rate is increased, there is an increase in the volume of the boiler water. This increase, which is known as *swell*, occurs because there is an increase in the number and size of the steam bubbles in the water. As the firing rate is decreased, there is a decrease in the volume of the water. This decrease, which is known as *shrink*, occurs because there are fewer steam bubbles and they are of smaller size. For any given weight of boiler water, the volume varies with the rate of combustion.

The problem of swell and shrink becomes even more complex

when we remember that the evaporation rate also increases as the firing rate increases and decreases as the firing rate decreases. When the firing rate is increased, therefore, the checkman must remember to feed *more* water to the boiler, even though the water level has already risen shortly because of swell. On the other hand, the checkman must remember to feed *less* water to the boiler when the firing rate is decreased, even though the water level has already dropped. Because these actions may appear to be contrary to common sense to a person who does not understand the concept of swell and shrink, a good deal of training is usually required before a man can be considered qualified to stand a check watch.

The control of combustion involves the control of fuel and the control of combustion air. There are three ways in which the firing rate may be increased or decreased in order to meet changes in steam demand: (1) by increasing or decreasing the fuel pressure, (2) by increasing or decreasing the number of burners in use, and (3) by changing the size of the sprayer plates in the atomizer assemblies. With every change, the amount of combustion air supplied to the boiler must also be changed in order to maintain the proper relationship between fuel and combustion air. The burnerman and the blowerman must therefore work very closely together in order to provide efficient combustion in the boiler furnace.

The burnerman cuts burners in and out and adjusts the oil pressure as necessary to keep the steam pressure at the required value. The burnerman is guided by the steam drum pressure gage. Also, he watches the annunciator which shows the signals going from the bridge to the engine-room, and in this way he can tell what steam demands are going to be made.

On a double-furnace boiler, there were two burnermen—one for the saturated side and one for the superheater side. The burnerman on the superheater side cuts burners in and out and adjusts fuel pressure to keep the superheater outlet temperature at the required value. The distant-reading thermometer that indicates the temperature of the steam at the super-heater outlet guides the burnerman on the superheater side. In addition, he had to keep a close check on the actions of the saturated-side burnerman so that he will always know how many burners are in use on the saturated side.

When two boilers are furnishing steam to the same engine, the burnermen of both boilers must work together to see that the load is equally divided between the two boilers.

The blowerman is responsible for operating the forced draft blowers that supply combustion air to the boiler. Although the air pressure in the double casings is affected by the number of registers in use and by the extent to which each register is open, it is chiefly determined by the manner in which the forced draft blowers are operated. The opening, setting, or adjusting of the air registers is the burnerman's job; the control of the forced draft blowers is the blowerman's job. As may be apparent, the burnerman and the blowerman must each know what the other man is doing at all times. The blowerman must always increase the air pressure before the burnerman increases the rate of combustion, and the burnerman must always decrease the rate of combustion before the blowerman decreases the air pressure.

If a boiler were not being supplied with sufficient air for combustion, everyone in the fireroom would have known about it immediately. The boiler will begin to pant and vibrate, and the fireroom force will receive complaints of "heavy black smoke" from the bridge. If the boiler was being supplied with too much air—that is, more excess air than was required for efficient combustion—the fireroom force may or may not know about it immediately. White smoke coming from the smokepipe is always an indication of large amounts of excess air. However, a perfectly clear smokepipe may be deceiving; it may mean that the boiler is operating with only a small amount of excess air, but it may also mean that as much as 300 percent excess air is causing enormous heat losses. The blowerman had to learn by experience how much air pressure should have been shown on the air pressure gage for all the various combinations of different numbers of burners, different sizes of sprayer plates, and different fuel pressures.

The number of men assigned to operate the fireroom auxiliary machinery varied from one ship to another, depending upon the size of the ship and the number of men available. Some ships may have had two or more men assigned to this duty; on other ships, the work may have been done by the petty officer in charge of the watch or by the messenger. The burnerman and the blowerman may have also take care of some of the auxiliaries. The checkman was never given any duties other than his primary ones of watching and maintaining the water level.

All fireroom operations were supervised and coordinated by the petty officer in charge of the watch. The petty officer in charge of the watch supervised all lighting off, operating, and securing procedures. He kept the engine-room and the engineering officer of the watch informed of operating conditions when necessary. He had to be constantly alert to the slightest indication of trouble and must be constantly prepared to deal with any casualty that may have occurred. The petty officer in charge of the watch was responsible for making sure that all safety precautions were being observed and that unsafe operating conditions were not allowed to exist.

Fireroom Efficiency

The military value of a naval vessel depends in large measure upon her cruising radius, which, in turn, depends upon the efficiency with which the engineering plant is operated. Perhaps the largest single factor in determining the efficiency of the engineering plant is the efficiency with which the boilers are operated. Greater savings in fuel, with consequent increase in steaming radius of the ship, may often be made in the fireroom than in all the rest of the engineering plant put together.

The *capacity* of a boiler was defined as the maximum rate at which the boiler can generate steam. The rate of steam generation is usually expressed in terms of pounds of water evaporated per hour. You should know something of the limitations upon boiler capacity, the significance of full-power and overload ratings, and the procedure for checking on boiler loads.

The capacity of any boiler was limited by three factors that have to do both with the design of the boiler and with its operation. These limitations, which are known as *end points*, are (1) the end point for *combustion*, (2) the end point for *moisture carryover*, and (3) the end point for *water circulation.*

Boilers were designed so that the end point for combustion should occur at a lower rate of steam generation than the end point for moisture carryover, and the end point for moisture carryover at a lower rate than the end point for water circulation. Since the end point for combustion occurs first, it is the only end point that is likely to be reached in a properly designed and properly operated boiler. However, it should be understood that it is quite possible to reach the end points for moisture carryover and water circulation *before* reaching the end point for combustion, by using larger sprayer plates than those recommended by the manufacturer or by the then Bureau of Ships. In such a case, the boiler might have suffered great damage before the end point for combustion was reached.

End Point for Combustion

The process of burning fuel in a boiler furnace involved forcing the fuel into the furnace at the proper viscosity through atomizers which break up the oil into a fog-like spray, and forcing air into the furnace in such a way that it mixed thoroughly with the oil spray. The amount of fuel that can be burned is limited primarily by the actual capacity of the equipment that supplies the fuel (including the capacity of the sprayer plates), by the amount of air that can be forced into the furnace, and by the ability of the burner apparatus to mix this air with the fuel. The volume and shape of the furnace are also limiting factors.

The end point for *combustion* for a boiler is reached when the capacity of the sprayer plates, at the designed pressure for the system, is reached or when the maximum amount of air that can be forced into the furnace is insufficient for complete combustion of the fuel. If the end point for combustion is actually reached because of insufficient air, the smoke in the uptakes will be black because it will contain particles of unburned fuel. However, this condition was rare, since the end point for combustion was artificially limited by sprayer plate capacity when the fuel was supplied at the burner manifold at designed operating pressure. As previously noted, this artificial limitation upon combustion in the boiler furnace was the factor that caused the end point for combustion to occur before either of the other two end points.

End Point for Moisture Carryover

The rate of steam generation should never be increased to the point at which an excessive amount of *moisture* is *carried over* in the steam. In general, naval specifications limited the allowable moisture content of steam leaving the saturated steam outlet to 1/4 of 1 percent.

Excessive carryover can be extremely damaging to piping, valves, and turbines, as well as to the superheater of the boiler. It is not only the moisture itself that is damaging but also the insoluble matter that may be carried in the moisture. This insoluble matter can form scale on superheater tubes, turbine blades, piping and fittings; in some cases, it may be sufficient to cause unbalance of rotating parts.

As the evaporation rate is increased, the amount of moisture carryover tends to increase also, due to the increased release of steam bubbles. Because naval boilers during the 1960s and 1970s were designed for high evaporation rates, steam separators and various baffle arrangements were used in the steam drum to separate moisture from the steam.

End Point for Water Circulation

In natural circulation boilers, circulation is dependent upon the difference between the density of the ascending mixture of hot water and steam and the density of the descending body of relatively cool water. As the firing rate is increased, the amount of heat transferred to the tubes is also increased. A greater number of tubes carry the upward flow of water and steam, and fewer tubes are left for the downward flow of water. Without downcomers to ensure a downward flow of water, a point would eventually be reached at which the downward flow would be insufficient to balance the upward flow of water and steam, and some tubes would become overheated and burn out. This condition would determine the end point for *water circulation.*

The use of downcomers ensures that the end point for water circulation will not be reached merely because the firing rate is increased.

Other factors that influence the circulation in a natural circulation boiler was the location of the burners, the arrangement of baffles in the tube banks, and the arrangement of tubes in the tube banks.

Full-power and overload ratings for the boilers in each ship were specified in the manufacturer's technical manual. The total quantity of steam required to develop contract shaft horsepower of the ship, divided by the number of boilers installed, gave boiler full-power capacity. Boiler overload capacity was usually 120 percent of boiler full-power capacity. For some boilers, a specific assigned maximum firing rate was designated.

A boiler should have not been forced beyond full-power capacity—that is, it should not have been steamed at a rate greater than that required to obtain full-power speed with all the ship's boilers in use. A boiler should have never been steamed beyond its overload capacity, or fired beyond the assigned maximum firing rate, except in dire emergency.

Checking Boiler Efficiency

In order to check on boiler efficiency it was necessary to compare the amount of fuel actually burned in a boiler with the amount that should be burned. This check was usually made during economy runs and during full-power runs. As a rule, 4 hours was allowed for each run. During the run, fuel consumption was measured at intervals of precisely 1 hour. This measure, when corrected for meter error and verified by tank soundings, gave the amount of fuel that was *actually* used.

The amount of fuel that should have been used under specified conditions may have been taken from tables or curves supplied in the manufacturer's technical manual for the boilers or from the ship's fuel performance tables. Since these two sources gave different figures for the amount of oil that should have been burned under various conditions, it was necessary to make a clear distinction between them. Incidentally, the differences arise from the fact that there are two basic approaches to the problem of checking on fuel consumption. When only concerned with boiler performance, there is only the use of the tables and charts from the manufacturer's technical manual; but when concerned with plant performance with respect to fuel consumption, the ship's fuel performance tables are used.

Boiler Casualty Control

Many fireroom casualties require knowledge of preventive measures and corrective measures. Some are major, some are minor; but all can be serious. In the event of a casualty, the principal doctrine to be impressed upon operating personnel is the prevention of additional or major casualties. Under normal operating conditions, the safety of personnel and machinery should be given first consideration. Therefore, it is necessary to know instantly and accurately what to do for each casualty. Stopping to find out exactly what must be done for each casualty could mean loss of life, extensive damage to machinery, and even complete failure of the engineering plant. A fundamental principle of engineering casualty control is split-plant operation. The purpose of split-plant design is to minimize the damage that might result from any one casualty that affects propulsion power, steering, and electrical power generation.

Although speed in controlling a casualty is essential, action should never be taken without accurate information; otherwise, the casualty may be mishandled, and further damage to the machinery may result. Cross-connecting and intact engineering plant with a partly damaged one must be delayed until it is certain that such action will not jeopardize the intact one.

Cross-connecting valves are provided for the main and auxiliary steam systems and other engineering systems so that any boiler or group of boilers, either forward or aft, may supply steam to each engine-room.

The discussion of fireroom casualties in this chapter was intended to give you an overall view of how casualties were handled. For further information on casualty control, the Naval Ship's Technical Manual, Chapter 9880, and the casualty control instructions issued for each type of ship were studied.

Most of the casualties discussed in this chapter were usually treated in a systematic procedure, but it is beyond the scope of this chapter to give each step in handling each casualty. In the step-by-step procedure one step was performed, then another, and so forth. In handling actual casualties, however, this systematic approach will have to be modified. Different circumstances required a different sequence of steps for control of a casualty. In addition, in handling real casualties several steps had to be performed at the same time. For example, main control had to be notified of any casualty to the boilers or to associated equipment. If "Notify main control" was listed as the third step in controlling a particular casualty, does this mean that the main control was not notified until the first two steps have been completed? Not at all. Notifying main control was a step that could usually be taken at the same time other steps were being taken. It was very helpful to learn the steps for controlling casualties in the order in which they were given; without overlooking the fact that the steps had to be performed simultaneously.

Feed Water Casualties

Casualties in the control of water level include low water, high water, feed pump casualties, loss of feed suction, and low feed pressure. These casualties are some of the most serious ones.

Low water is one of the most serious of all fireroom casualties. Low water may be caused by failure of the feed pumps, ruptures in the feed discharge line, defective check valves, low water in the feed tank, or other defects.

However, the most frequent cause of low water is inattention on the part of the checkman and the petty officer in charge of the watch, or the diversion of their attention to other duties. The checkman's sole responsibility is to keep the water in the boiler at a proper level.

Low water is extremely damaging to the boiler and may endanger the lives of fireroom personnel. When the furnace is hot and there is insufficient water to absorb the heat, the heating surfaces are likely to be distorted, the brickwork damaged, and the boiler casing warped by the excessive heat. In addition, serious steam and water leaks may occur because of low water.

Disappearance of the water level from the water gage glasses had to be treated as a casualty requiring the *immediate* securing of the boiler!

It should be noted that when the water level fell low enough to uncover portions of the tubes, the heat transfer surface was reduced. As a rule, therefore, the steam pressure will drop. Ordinarily a drop in steam pressure is the result of an increased demand for steam, and the natural tendency is to cut in more burners to fulfill the demand. If the drop in steam pressure is caused by low water, however, increasing the firing rate will result in serious damage to the boiler and possibly in injury to fireroom personnel. The possibility that a drop in steam pressure indicates low water had to always be kept in mind. Personnel always checked the level in the water gage glasses before cutting in additional burners, when steam pressure had dropped for no apparent reason.

High water was another serious casualty that was most frequently caused by the inattention of the checkman and the petty officer in charge of the watch. If the water level in the gage glass went above the highest visible part, the boiler had to be secured *immediately.*

By careful observation, it was sometimes possible to distinguish between an empty gage glass and a full one by the presence or absence of condensate trickling down the inside of the glass. The presence of condensate indicated an empty glass—that is, a low water casualty. However, the boiler had to be secured whether the water was high or low. After the boiler had been secured, the location of the water level could be determined by using the gage glass cutout valves and drain valves.

Failure of a *feed system pump* can have drastic consequences. Unless the pump casualty is corrected immediately, the pump failure will lead to low water in the boiler. In addition to the obvious dangers associated with low water, some are equally serious but not so obvious. For example, low water causes complete or partial loss of steam pressure. When steam pressure is lost or greatly reduced, you will lose the services of vital auxiliary machinery—pumps, blowers, and so forth. It is essential, therefore, that feed pump casualties be handled rapidly and correctly.

If the *main feed pump discharge pressure* is too low, the first three things to be checked are (1) the feed booster pump discharge pressure, (2) the level and pressure in the deaerating feed tank, and (3) the feed stop and check valves on idle boilers. A failure of the feed booster pump will, of course, cause loss of suction and, therefore, loss of discharge pressure of the main feed pump. If the feed stop and check valves on idle boilers have accidentally been left open, the main feed pump discharge pressure may be low merely because water has been pumped to an idle boiler, as well as to the steaming boiler.

Some of the most likely causes of failure of the main feed pump are (1) malfunction of the constant-pressure pump governor, (2) and air-bound or vapor-bound condition of the main feed pump, (3) faulty pump clearances, and (4) malfunction or improper setting of the speed-limiting governor.

In many installations, the feed booster pump and the main feed pump were in the engine-room. In other installations, the feed booster pump was in the engine-room but the main feed pump was in the fireroom. In this latter type of installation, *failure of the feed booster pump* was indicated to the fireroom force by loss of main feed pump discharge pressure and by the sounding of the low-pressure feed alarm that was usually fitted where this type of machinery arrangement exists. Engine-room personnel dealt with the casualty to the feed booster pump, if the pump was in the engine-room; but fireroom personnel had to take immediate action to maintain a supply of feed water to the boiler.

If the engine-room was unable to remedy the situation immediately, they started the emergency feed pump on *cold suction*. The emergency feed pump could take a *hot suction* from the feed booster pump, or a cold suction from the reserve feed tanks. In standby condition, this pump was always lined up on cold suction.

If the *main feed pump* failed and there was no standby pump available, they started the emergency feed pump on hot suction and continue to feed the boiler. If the feed also failed then it was necessary to start the emergency feed pump on cold suction.

If the *emergency feed pump* failed, the procedures for handling the casualty varied according to the situation existing at the time of the failure.

In many ships, the emergency feed pump was normally used for in-port operation, with the main feed pump in standby condition and the feed booster pump providing a hot suction for the emergency feed pump. Under these conditions, emergency feed pump failure was handled by notifying the engine-room so that the main feed pump could be put on the line and used to feed the boiler.

A more difficult problem arose if the emergency feed pump failed when it was being used because of a previous casualty to the feed booster pump or to the main feed pump. Under these conditions, it may have been possible to deal with the situation by cross-connecting and using a pump in some other space to supply feed to the boiler. If the operating conditions did not allow this solution to the problem, it was necessary to secure the boiler immediately in order to prevent a low water casualty.

Fuel System Casualties

Casualties to any part of the fuel oil system are serious and must be remedied at once. Common casualties included (1) oil in the fuel oil heater drains, (2) water in the fuel oil, (3) loss of fuel oil suction, (4) failure of the fuel oil service pump, and (5) fuel oil leaks. It should be noted that these casualties to the fuel oil system were for ships burning NSFO. The procedures for ships burning other types of fuel differed to some extent, but not in all cases.

Oil leakage from the fuel oil heaters into the drains may cause oil contamination of the drain lines; the reserve feed tanks, the deaerating feed tank, and the feed system piping and pumps. The presence of oil in any part of the feed system is dangerous because of the possibility that the oil will eventually reach the boilers, where it will cause steaming difficulties and serious damage to the boilers.

Fuel oil heater drains had to be inspected hourly for the presence of oil.

The presence of an appreciable amount of *water in the fuel oil* is indicated by hissing and sputtering of the fires and atomizers and by racing of the fuel oil service pump. The situation must be remedied at once; otherwise, choked atomizers, loss of fires, flarebacks, and refractory damage may result.

A loss of fuel oil suction usually indicates that the oil in the service suction tank has dropped below the level of the fuel oil service pump suction line. This causes a mixture of air and oil to be pumped to the atomizers. The atomizers begin to hiss and the fuel oil service pump begins to race. It must be strongly emphasized that the loss of fuel oil suction can cause serious results. Related casualties may include loss of auxiliary steam and electric power, with the complete loss of all electrically driven and steam-driven machinery.

Failure of the fuel oil service pump can cause the same progressive series of casualties as those that result from loss of fuel oil suction.

Fuel oil leaks are very serious, no matter how small they may be. Fuel oil vapors are very explosive. Any oil spillage or leakage must be wiped up immediately.

Flarebacks

A *flareback* likely occurred whenever the pressure in the furnace shortly exceeds the pressure in the boiler air casing. Flarebacks were caused by an inadequate air supply for the amount of oil being supplied, or by a delay in lighting the mixture of air and oil.

Situations which commonly led to flarebacks included: (1) attempting to light off or to relight burners from hot brickwork; (2) gunfire or bombing which creates a partial vacuum at the blower intake, thus reducing the air pressure supplied by the blowers; (3) forced draft blower failure; (4) accumulation of unburned fuel oil or combustible gases in furnaces, tube banks, uptakes, or air casings; and (5) any event which first extinguishes the burners and then allows unburned fuel oil to spray out into the hot furnace. An example of this last situation might be a temporary interruption of the fuel supply, which would cause the burners to go out; when the fuel oil supply returns to normal, the heat of the furnace might not be sufficient to relight the burners immediately.

In a few seconds, however, the fuel oil sprayed into the furnace would be vaporized, and a flareback or even an explosion might result.

Superheater Casualties

If the distant-reading superheater thermometer did not register a normal increase in temperature when the superheater was first lighted off, the trouble may have been either lack of steam flow or failure of the distant-reading thermometer. Lack of steam flow had to be considered as a possible cause even if the superheater steam flow indicator (if installed) showed that there was a flow. If the thermometer did not register a normal increase in temperature, all superheater burners were secured.

When operating with superheat, it was essential to keep a constant check on the flow of steam through the superheater and on the superheater outlet temperature. Any deviation from normal conditions had to be corrected immediately.

It is important to remember that a casualty to some other part of the engineering plant would have reduced or entirely stopped the flow of steam through the superheater, and so caused a superheater casualty, unless appropriate action was taken to prevent damage. For example, a casualty to the main engines might have called for a sudden large reduction or even a complete stoppage of steam flow. Even if the superheater burners were secured, there was still a need for steam flow to protect the superheater from the heater of the furnace. In this event, or whenever a greater flow was required than could be obtained by ordinary means, the superheater safety valves had to be lifted by hand to ensure a positive flow of steam through the superheater .

When the superheater thermal alarm sounds, the superheater fires must be immediately decreased to bring the temperature below alarm temperature. Do *not* decrease the temperature further than necessary. It is very seldom necessary to secure all superheater burners in order to bring the temperature down to the prescribed point.

Casualties to Refractories

If brick or plastic falls out of the furnace walls and goes unnoticed, burned casings may result. If brick or plastic falls out of a furnace wall, if practicable, secure all the burners. If it is not practicable to secure all the burners, those burners that are adjacent to the damaged section had to be secured.

Note: It was sometimes necessary to continue operating the boiler until another boiler can be brought in on the line.

Casualties to Boiler Pressure Parts

When *boiler pressure parts*, such as tubes, carry away or rupture, escaping steam may have caused serious injury to personnel and damage to the boiler. It was urgent that the boiler be secured, relieved of its pressure, and cooled until no more steam was generated. If a boiler pressure part carried away or ruptured, steps were taken immediately upon discovery of the casualty, to minimize and localize the damage as much as circumstances would allow.

Gage glasses were connected to the water and steam spaces of the steam drum. If a water gage glass carries away, the mixture of steam and water escaping from the gage connections may have seriously burned personnel in the area. A ball check valve in the high-pressure gage line functions when the flow was excessive. In addition, the hazard of flying particles of glass made this casualty very serious. The particles of glass could lodge in your eyes and blind you, or they could lodge elsewhere in your body and cause serious injury. If a gage glass casualty occurred, personnel threw a large sheet of asbestos cloth, rubber matting, or similar material over the glass. Then took immediate action to secure the gage glass.

Precautions to Prevent Fires

The following precautions had to be taken to prevent fires:

1. Do not allow oil to accumulate in any place. Particular care must be taken to guard against oil accumulation in drip pans under pumps, in bilges, in the furnaces, on the floor plates, and in the bottom of air-encased boilers. Should leakage from the oil system to the fireroom occur at anytime, immediate action should be taken to shut off the oil supply by means of quick-closing valves and to stop the oil pump.

2. Tight joints in all oil lines are essential to safety. Immediate steps must be taken to stop leaks whenever they are discovered. Flange safety shields should be installed on all flanges in fuel oil service lines to prevent spraying oil on adjacent hot surfaces.

3. No lights should be permitted in the fireroom except electric lights (fitted with steam-tight globes, or lenses, and wire guards), and permanently fitted smoke indicator and water gage lights. If work is being done in the vicinity of flammable vapors, or if rust-preventive compound or metal-conditioning compound is being used, all portable lights should be of the explosion proof type.

Boiler Maintenance

The engineer officer had to keep himself fully acquainted with the general condition of each boiler and the manner in which each was being operated and maintained. He had to satisfy himself, by periodic inspections, that the exterior and interior surfaces of the boiler were clean; that the refractory linings adequately protected the casing, drums, and headers; that the integrity of the pressure parts were being maintained; and that the operating condition of the burners, safety valves, operating instruments, and other boiler appurtenances were satisfactory.

The engineer officer also had to assure himself that the idle boilers were properly secured at all times, and while steaming, the fuel oil used was free of sea water, and the feed water was within prescribed limits, free of salts, entrained oxygen, and oil.

All parts of the boiler had to be carefully examined whenever they were exposed for cleaning and overhauling, and the conditions observed had to be described in the boiler record sheet and the engineering log. All unusual cases of damage or deterioration discovered at any time were reported to the type commander, stating in detail the extent of injury sustained, remedies applied, and the causes, if determined. If considered of sufficient importance or technical assistance was desired from the Naval Ship Systems Command, a copy of the correspondence was forwarded.

The requirements for fireroom maintenance and repair were established by the Planned Maintenance Subsystem; information on this system was contained in the then Maintenance and Material Management (3-M) Manual, OPNAV 43P2 Revised edition (currently OPNAVINST 4790.1 series). All fireroom maintenance was conducted in accordance with this system.

CHAPTER 3

DIESEL AND GASOLINE ENGINE PLANTS

Much of the machinery and equipment discussed in the preceding chapters utilizes steam as the working fluid in the process of converting thermal energy to mechanical energy. This chapter deals with internal combustion engines, in which air (or a mixture of air and fuel) serves as the working fluid. The internal combustion engines considered are those to which the thermodynamic cycles of the open and *heated engine* types apply. In engines that operate on these cycles, the working fluid is taken into the engine, heat is added to the fluid, the energy available in the fluid is utilized, and then the fluid is discarded. During the process, thermal energy is converted to mechanical energy. The purpose of this chapter is to present the basic theory and the fundamental principles underlying the energy conversion in internal combustion engines, and the functions of the engine parts, accessories, and systems essential for the conversion. No attempt is made to describe design, construction, models, etc., except as necessary to make the theory of operation and the function of components readily understandable.

Internal combustion engines are used extensively in the Navy, serving as propulsion units in a variety of installations such as ships, boats, airplanes, and automotive vehicles. Engines of the internal combustion type are also used as prime movers for auxiliary machinery. Internal combustion engines in a majority of the shipboard installations are of the reciprocating type. In the 1970s through 1980s, engines of the gas turbine type have been placed in Navy service as power plants. Gas turbine engines are discussed in chapter 4 of this text.

RECIPROCATING ENGINES

Most of the internal combustion engines in marine installations of the Navy are of the reciprocating type. This classification is because the cylinders in which the energy conversion takes place are fitted with pistons, which employ a reciprocating motion. Internal combustion engines of the reciprocating type are commonly identified as diesel and gasoline engines. The general trend in navy service is to install diesel engines rather than gasoline engines unless special conditions favor the use of the latter.

Most of the information on reciprocating engines in this chapter applies to diesel and gasoline engines. However, these engines differ in some respects; the principal differences that exist are noted and discussed.

Basic Principles

The operation of an internal combustion engine of the reciprocating type involves the admission of fuel and air into a combustion space and the compression and ignition of the charge. The resulting combustion releases gases and increases the temperature within the space. As temperature increases, pressure increases and forces the piston to move. This movement is transmitted through a chain of parts to a shaft. The resulting rotary motion of the shaft is utilized for work and heat energy is transformed into mechanical energy. In order for the process to be continuous, the expanded gases must be removed from the combustion space, a new charge admitted, and then the process repeated.

In the study of engine operating principles, starting with the admission of air and fuel and following through to the removal of the expanded gases, it will be noted that a series of events takes place. The term cycle identifies the sequence of events that takes place in the cylinder of an engine for each power impulse transmitted to the crankshaft. These events always occur in the same order each time the cycle is repeated. The number of events occurring in a cycle of operation will depend upon the engine type—diesel or gasoline.

The events and their sequence in a cycle operation for a:

Diesel Engine	**Gasoline Engine**
Intake of air *Compression* of air	*Intake* of fuel and air *Compression* of fuel-air mixture
Injection of fuel	*Ignition* and *Combustion* of charge
Ignition and *Combustion* of charge	*Expansion* of gases
Expansion of gases	*Removal* of waste
Removal of waste	

The principal difference, as shown above, in the cycles of operation for diesel and gasoline engines involves the admission of fuel and air to the cylinder. While this takes place as one event in the operating cycle of a gasoline engine, it involves two events in diesel engines. Insofar as events are concerned, there are six main events taking place in the diesel cycle of operation and five in the cycle of a gasoline engine. This is pointed out in order to emphasize the fact that the events that take place and the piston strokes that occur during a cycle of operation are not identical. Even though the events of a cycle are closely related to piston position and movement, all of the events will take place during the cycle regardless of the number of piston strokes involved. The relationship of events and piston strokes is discussed later under a separate heading.

The mechanics of engine operation is sometimes referred to as the *mechanical* or *operating cycle* of an engine; while the heat process that produces the forces that move engine parts may be referred to as the *combustion cycle*. A cycle of each type is included in a cycle of engine operation.

Mechanical Cycles

In the preceding section, the events taking place in a cycle of engine operation were emphasized. Little was said about piston strokes except that a complete sequence of events would occur during a cycle regardless of the number of strokes made by the piston. The number of piston strokes occurring during any one series of events is limited to either two or four, depending upon the design of the engine; thus, the 4-stroke cycle and the 2-stroke cycle. These cycles are known as the mechanical cycles of operation.

Four- and Two-Stroke Cycles

Both types of mechanical cycles are used in diesel and gasoline engines. However, most large gasoline engines in Navy service operate on the 4-stoke cycle; a greater number of diesel engines operate on the 2-stroke than on the 4-stroke cycle. The relationship of the events and piston strokes occurring in a cycle of operation involves some of the differences between the 2-stroke cycle and the 4-stroke cycle.

Relationship of Events and Strokes in a Cycle

A piston stroke is the distance a piston moves between limits of travel. The cycle of operation is an engine operating on the 4-stroke cycle involves four piston strokes—in-take, *compression, power,* and *exhaust.* In the case of the 2-stroke cycle, only two strokes apply— *power* and *compression.*

A check of the previous table listing the series of events, which take place during the cycles of operation of diesel and gasoline engines, will show that the strokes are named to correspond to some of the events. However, since six events are listed for diesel engines and five events for gasoline engines, it is evident that more than one event takes place during some of the strokes, especially in the case of the 2-stroke cycle. Even though this is the case, it is common practice to identify some of the events as strokes of the piston. This is because such events as intake, compression, power and exhaust in a 4-stroke cycle involve at least a major portion of a stroke and, in some cases, more than one stroke. The same is true of power and compression events and strokes in a 2-stroke cycle. Such association of events and strokes overlooks other events taking place during a cycle of operation. This oversight sometimes leads to confusion when the operating principles of an engine are being considered.

This discussion points out the relationship of events to strokes by covering the number of events occurring during a specific stroke, the duration of an event with respect to a piston stroke, and the cases where one event overlaps another. The relationship of events to strokes is more readily understood, if the movements of a piston and its crankshaft are considered first. When at the top of a stroke, the piston position is located at the top of a circle. When the piston is at the bottom of a stroke, the piston position is located at the bottom center of the circle. When the piston is at top center, upward motion has stopped and downward motion is ready to start or, with respect to motion, the piston is "dead."

The points that designate changes in direction of motion for a piston and crank are commonly called *top dead center* (TDC) and *bottom dead center* (BDC). TDC and BDC should be kept in mind since they identify the start and end of a *stroke* and they are the points from which the start and end of *events* are established.

By following the strokes and events, it can be noted that the intake event starts before TDC, or before the actual down stroke (intake) starts, and continues on past BDC, or beyond the end of the stroke. The compression event starts when the intake event ends, but the upstroke (compression) has been in process since BDC. The injection and ignition events overlap with the latter part of the compression event, which ends at TDC. The burning of the fuel continues a few degrees past TDC. The power event or expansion of gases ends several degrees before the down (power) stroke ends at BDC. The exhaust event starts when the power event ends and continues through the complete upstroke (exhaust) and past TDC. Note the overlap of the exhaust event with the intake event of the next cycle. The details on why certain events overlap and why some events are shorter or longer with respect to strokes will be covered later in this chapter.

From the preceding discussion, it can be seen why the term "stroke" is sometimes used to identify an event that occurs in a cycle of operation. However, it is best to keep in mind that a stoke involves 180° of crankshaft rotation (or piston movement between dead centers) while the corresponding event may take place during a greater or lesser number of degrees of shaft rotation.

The relationship of events to strokes in a 2-stroke cycle diesel engine reveals a number of differences between the two types of mechanical or operating cycles. These differences are not too difficult to understand if one keeps in mind that four piston strokes and 720° of crankshaft rotation are involved in the 4-stroke cycle while only half as many strokes and degrees are involved in a 2-stroke cycle. Even though the two piston strokes are frequently referred to as power and compression, they are identified as the "down stroke" (TDC to BDC) and "up stroke" (BDC to TDC) in this discussion in order to avoid confusion when reference is made to an event.

Starting with the admission of air, the piston is in the lower half of the down stroke and the exhaust event is in process. The exhaust event started a number of degrees before intake, both starting several degrees before the piston reached BDC. The overlap of these events is necessary in order that the incoming air can aid in clearing the cylinder of exhaust gases. Note that the exhaust event stops a few degrees before the intake event stops, but several degrees after the upstroke of the piston has started. (The exhaust event in some 2-stroke cycle diesel engines ends a few degrees after the intake event ends). When the scavenging event ends, the cylinder is charged with the air, which is to be compressed. The compression event takes place during the major portion of the upstroke. The injection event, ignition and combustion occur during the latter part of the upstroke. (The point at which the injection ends varies with engines. In some cases, it ends before TDC; in others, a few degrees after TDC). The intense heat generated during the compression of the air ignites the fuel-air mixture and the pressure resulting from combustion forces the piston down. The expansion of the gases continues through a major portion of the down stroke. After the force of the gases has been expended, the exhaust valve opens and permits the burned gases to enter the exhaust manifold. As the piston moves downward, the intake ports are uncovered and the incoming air clears the cylinder of the remaining exhaust gases and fills the cylinder with a fresh air charge, the cycle of operation has started again.

Now what is the difference between the 2- and 4-stroke cycles? From the standpoint of the mechanics of operation, the principal difference is in the number of piston strokes taking place during the cycle of events. A more significant difference is the fact that a 2-stroke cycle engine delivers twice as many power impulses to the crankshaft for every 720° of shaft rotation.

Any diagrams showing the mechanical cycles of operation in

gasoline engines would be somewhat similar to those described for diesel engines except that there would be one less event taking place during the gasoline engine cycle. Since air and fuel are admitted to the cylinder of a gasoline engine as a mixture during the intake event, the injection event does not apply.

The exact number of degrees before or after TDC or BDC that an event starts and ends will vary between engines. Information on such details should be obtained from appropriate technical manuals dealing with the specific engine in question.

Combustion Cycles

To this point, the strokes of a piston and the related events taking place during a cycle of operation have been given greater consideration than the heat process involved in the cycle. However, the mechanics of engine operation cannot be discussed without dealing with heat. Such terms as ignition, combustion, and expansion of gases, all indicate that heat is essential to a cycle of engine operation. So far, particular differences between diesel and gasoline engines have not been pointed out, except the number of events occurring during the cycle of operation. Whether a diesel engine or a gasoline engine, the 2- or the 4-stroke cycle may apply. Then, one of the principal differences between these types of engines must involve the heat process utilized to produce the forces which make the engine operate. The heat processes are sometimes called combustion or heat cycles.

The three most common combustion cycles associated with reciprocating internal combustion engines are the *Otto cycle*, the *true diesel* cycle, and the *modified diesel cycle.*

Reference to combustion cycles suggests another important difference between gasoline and diesel engines—compression pressure. This factor is directly related to the combustion process utilized in an engine. Diesel engines have a much higher compression pressure than gasoline engines. The higher compression pressure in diesels explains the difference in the methods of ignition used in gasoline and diesel engines. Compressing the gases within a cylinder raises the temperature of the confined gases. The greater the compression, the higher the temperature. In a gasoline engine, the compression temperature is always lower than the point where the fuel would ignite spontaneously. Thus, the heat required to ignite the fuel must come from an external source—spark ignition. On the other hand, the compression temperature in a diesel engine is far above the ignition point of the fuel oil; therefore, ignition takes place as a result heat generated by compression of the air within the cylinder—compression ignition.

The difference in the methods of ignition indicates that there is a basic difference in the combustion cycles upon which diesel and gasoline engines operate. This difference involves the behavior of the combustion gases under varying conditions of pressure, temperature, and volume. Since this is the case, the relationship of these factors is considered before the combustion cycles.

Relationship of Temperature, Pressure, and Volume

The relationship of these three conditions as found in an engine can be illustrated by considering what takes place in a cylinder fitted with a reciprocating piston.

Instruments are provided which indicate the pressure within the cylinder and the temperature inside and outside the cylinder. Consider that the air in the cylinder is at atmospheric pressure and that the temperatures, inside and outside the cylinder, are about 70°F.

If the cylinder is an airtight container and a force pushes the piston toward the top of the cylinder, the entrapped charge will be compressed. As the compression progresses, the volume of the air *decreases*, the *pressure increases*, and the *temperature rises*. These changing conditions continue as the piston moves and when the piston nears TDC, there has been a marked decrease in volume and both pressure and temperature are much greater than at the beginning of compression. Note that pressure will have gone from to 470 psi and temperature will have increased from 70° to about 1,000° F, These changing conditions indicate that mechanical energy, in the form of work done on the piston, has been transformed into heat energy in the compressed air. The temperature of the air has been raised sufficiently to cause ignition of fuel injected into the cylinder.

Further changes take place after ignition. Since ignition occurs shortly before TDC, there is little change in volume until the piston passes TDC. However, there is a sharp increase in pressure and temperature shortly after ignition takes place. The increased pressure forces the piston downward. As the piston moves downward, the gases expand, or increase in volume, and pressure and temperature decrease rapidly. The changes in volume, pressure, and temperature, described, were representative of the changing conditions within the cylinder of the then modern diesel engine.

The changes in volume and pressure in an engine cylinder can be illustrated by diagrams. Such diagrams are made by devices which measure and record the pressures at various piston positions during a cycle of engine operation. Diagrams that show the relationship between pressures and corresponding piston positions are called *pressure-volume diagrams* or *indicator cards.*

On diagrams which provide a graphic representation of cylinder pressure as related to volume, the vertical line 'P' on the diagram represents pressure and the horizontal line 'V' represents volume. When a diagram is used as an indicator card, the pressure line is marked off in units of pressure and the volume line is marked off in inches. The volume line could be used to show the length of the piston stroke that is proportional to volume. The distance between adjacent letters on each of the diagrams represents an event of a combustion cycle—that is, compression of air, burning of the charge, expansion of gas, and removal of gases.

Otto (Constant-Volume) Cycle

In theory, this combustion cycle is one in which combustion, induced by spark ignition, occurs at constant volume. The Otto cycle and its principles serve as the basis for modern gasoline engine designs.

Compression of the charge in the cylinder is adiabatic. Spark ignition occurs, and, due to the volatility of the mixture, combustion practically amounts to an explosion. Combustion occurs (theoretically) just as the piston reaches TDC. During combustion, there is no piston travel; thus there is no change in the volume of the gas in the cylinder. This accounts for the descriptive term, *constant volume.* During combustion, there is a rapid rise of temperature followed by a pressure increase that performs the work during the expansion phase. The removal of gases is at constant volume.

True Diesel (Constant-Pressure) Cycle

This cycle may be defined as one in which combustion, induced by compression ignition, theoretically occurs at a constant pressure. Adiabatic compression of the air increases its temperature to a point where ignition occurs automatically when the fuel is injected. Fuel injection and combustion are so controlled as to give constant-pressure combustion. This is followed by adiabatic expansion and constant volume.

In the true diesel cycle, the burning of the mixture of fuel and compressed air is a relatively slow process when compared with the quick, explosive-type combustion process of the Otto cycle. The injected fuel penetrates the compressed air, some of the fuel ignites, and then the rest of the charge burns. The expansion of the gases keeps pace with the change in volume caused by piston travel; combustion is said to occur at constant pressure.

Modified Combustion Cycles

The preceding discussion covers the theoretical combustion cycles that serve as the basis for modern engines. In actual operation, modern engines operate on modifications of the theoretical cycles. However, characteristics of the true cycles are incorporated in the cycles of modern engines. This is pointed out in the following discussion of examples representing the actual cycles of operation in gasoline and diesel engines.

The following examples are based on the 4-stroke mechanical cycle since the majority of gasoline engines use this type of cycle; thus, a means of comparing the cycles found in both gasoline and diesel engines is provided. Differences existing in diesel engines operating on the 2-stroke cycle are pointed out.

In the case of Otto cycle, this event includes the admission of fuel and air. As indicated earlier, the intake event starts before TDC. Pressure is decreasing and after the piston reaches TDC and starts down, a vacuum is created which facilitates the flow of the fuel-air mixture into the cylinder. The intake event continues a few degrees past BDC. Since the piston is now on an upstroke, compression takes place and continues until the piston reaches TDC. This is an increase in pressure and the decrease in volume. Spark ignition starts combustion that takes place very rapidly. There is some change in volume since the phase starts before and ends after TDC.

There is a sharp increase in pressure during the combustion phase. The increase in pressure provides the force necessary to drive the piston down again. The gases continue to expand as the piston moves toward BDC, and the pressure decreases as the volume increases. The exhaust event starts a few degrees before BDC, and the pressure drops rapidly until the piston reaches BDC. As the piston moves toward TDC, there is a slight drop in pressure as the waste gases are discharged. The exhaust event continues a few degrees past TDC to point g so that the incoming charge aids in removing the remaining waste gases.

The modified diesel combustion cycle is one in which the combustion phase, induced by compression ignition, begins on a constant-volume basis and ends on a constant-pressure basis. In other words, the modified cycle is a combination of the Otto and true diesel cycles. The modified cycle is used as the basis for the design of practically all modern diesel engines.

By comparing the two, it will be found that the phases of the diesel cycle are relatively the same as those of the Otto cycle, except for the combustion phase. Fuel is injected and combustion is represented. While combustion in the Otto cycle is practically at constant-volume throughout the phase, combustion in the modified diesel cycle takes place with volume practically constant for a short time, during which period there is a sharp increase in pressure, until the piston reaches a point slightly past TDC. Then, combustion continues at a relatively constant pressure, dropping slightly as combustion ends. For these reasons, the combustion cycle in the diesel engines were sometimes referred to as the constant-volume constant-pressure cycle.

Pressure-volume diagrams for gasoline and diesel engines operating on the 2-stroke cycle would be similar to those just discussed, except that separate exhaust and intake curves would not exist. They do not exist because intake and exhaust occur during a relatively short interval of time near BDC and do not involve full strokes of the piston as in the case of the 4-stroke cycle. The exhaust and intake phases would take place between e and b with some overlap of the events.

The preceding discussion has pointed out some of the main differences between engines that operate on the Otto cycle and those that operate on the modified diesel cycle. In brief, these differences involve (1) the mixing of fuel and air, (2) compression ratio, (3) ignition, and (4) the combustion process.

Action of Combustion Gases on Pistons

During 1955 through 1990, engines were classified in many ways. Mention has already been made of some classifications such as those based on (1) the fuels used (diesel fuel and gasoline), (2) the ignition methods (spark and compression), (3) the combustion cycles (Otto and diesel), and (4) the mechanical cycles (2-stroke and 4-stroke). Engines may also be classified on the basis of cylinder arrangements (V, in-line, opposed, etc.), the cooling media (liquid and air), and the valve arrangements (L-head, valve-in head, etc.). The manner in which the pressure of combustion gases acts upon the piston to move it in the cylinder of an engine was also used as a method of classifying engines.

The classification of engines according to combustion-gas action was based on a consideration of whether the pressure created by the combustion gases acts upon one or two surfaces of a single piston or against single surfaces of two separate and opposed pistons. The two types of engines under this classification were commonly referred to as *single-acting* and opposed-piston engines.

Single-Acting Engines

Engines of this type are those which had one piston per cylinder and in which the pressure of combustion gases acts only on one surface of the piston. This is a feature of design rather than principle, for the basic principles of operation apply whether an engine is single acting, opposed piston, or double acting.

The pistons in most single-acting engines were of the trunk type (length greater than diameter). The barrel or wall of a piston of this type has one end closed (crown) and one end open (skirt end). Only the crown of a trunk piston served as part of the combustion space surface. Therefore, the pressure of combustion can act only against the crown; with respect to the surfaces of a piston, pressure is single acting. Most modern gasoline engines as well as many of the diesel engines used by the Navy are single acting.

Opposed-Piston Engines

With respect to combust ion-gas action, the term *opposed piston* is used to identify those engines which have two pistons and one combustion space in each cylinder. The pistons are arranged in "opposed" positions—that is, crown to crown, with the combustion space in between. When combustion takes place, the gases act against the crowns of both pistons, driving them in opposite directions. The term "opposed" not only signifies that, with respect to pressure and piston surfaces, the gases act in "opposite" direction, but also classifies piston arrangement within the cylinder.

The then modern engines which had the opposed-piston arrangement, two crankshafts (upper and lower) are required for transmission of power. Both shafts contributed to the power output of the engine. They were connected in one of two ways; chains as well as gears were used for the connection between shafts. However, in most opposed-piston engines that were common to Navy service, the crankshafts were connected by a vertical gear drive.

The cylinders of opposed-piston engines had scavenging air ports located near the top. These ports were opened and closed by the upper piston. Exhaust ports located near the bottom of the cylinder were closed and opened by the lower piston.

Movement of the opposed pistons is such that the crowns are closest together near the center of the cylinder. When at this position, the pistons are not at the true piston dead centers. This is because the lower crankshaft operates a few degrees in advance of the upper shaft. The number of degrees that a crank on the lower shaft travels in advance of a corresponding crank on the upper shaft is called *lower crank* lead.

Opposed-piston engines used by the Navy during 1955 through 1990 operated on the 2-stroke cycle. In engines of the opposed-piston type, as in 2-stroke cycle single-acting engines, there is an overlap of the various events occurring during a cycle of operation. Injection and the burning of the fuel start during the latter part of the compression event and extend into the power phase. There is also an overlap of the exhaust and scavenging periods.

Engines of the opposed-piston design have had a number of advantages over single-acting engines of comparable rating. Some of these advantages were less weight per horsepower developed; lack of cylinder heads and valve mechanisms (and the cooling and lubricating problems connected with them); and fewer moving parts.

Functions of Reciprocating Engine Components

The design of most internal combustion engines of the reciprocating type follows much the same general pattern. Though engines are not all exactly alike, there are certain features common to all, and the principal components of most engines are similarly arranged. Since the general structure of gasoline engines is basically the same as that of diesel engines, the following discussion of the engine components applies generally to both types of engines. However, differences do exist and these will be pointed out wherever applicable.

The principal components of an internal combustion engine may be divided into two principal groups—parts and systems. The main parts of an internal combustion engine may be further divided into structural parts and moving parts. Structural parts, for the purpose of this discussion, include those that, with respect to engine operation, do not involve motion; namely, the structural frame and its components and related parts. The other group of engine parts includes those that involve motion. Many of the principal parts that are mounted within the main structure of an engine are moving parts. Moving parts are considered as those that convert the power developed by combustion in the cylinder to the mechanical energy that is available for useful work at the output shaft.

The systems commonly associated with the engine proper are those necessary to make combustion possible, and those which minimize and dissipate heat created by combustion and friction. Since combustion requires air, fuel, and heat (ignition), systems providing each may be found on some engines. However, since a diesel engine generates its own heat for combustion within the cylinders, no separate ignition system is required for engines of this type. The problem of heat, created as a result of combustion and friction, is taken care of by two separate systems—cooling and lubrication. The functions of the parts and systems of engines, which operate on the principles already described, are discussed briefly in the following paragraphs.

Main Structural Parts

The main purpose of the structural parts of an engine is to maintain the moving parts in their proper relative position. This is necessary if the gas pressure produced by combustion is to fulfill its function.

The term *frame* is sometimes used to identify a single part of an engine; in other cases, it identifies several stationary parts fastened together to support most of the moving engine parts and engine accessories. For the purpose of this discussion, the latter meaning will be used. As the load-carrying part of the engine, the frame of the modern engine may include such parts as the cylinder block, crankcase, bedplate or base, sump or oil pan, and end plates.

The part of the engine frame that supports the engine's cylinder liners and head or heads is generally referred to as the *cylinder block*. The blocks for most large engines are of the welded-steel type construction. Blocks of small high-speed engines may be of the en bloc construction. In this type construction, the block is cast in one piece. Two types of cylinder blocks in Navy service are: blocks designed for some large engines with in-line cylinder arrangement and blocks constructed for some engines with V-type cylinder arrangement.

The engine frame part that serves as housing for the crankshaft is commonly called the *crankcase*. In some engines, the crankcase is an integral part of the cylinder block, requiring an oil pan, sump, or base to complete the housing. In others, the crankcase is a separate part and is bolted to the block.

In large engines of early design, the support for the main bearings was provided by a *bedplate*. The bedplate was bolted to the crankcase and an oil pan was bolted to the bedplate when a separate oil pan was used. In some large engines after the 1970s design, the support for main bearings was provided by a part called the *base*. This type base served as a combination bedplate and oil plan. This base requires the engine block to complete the frame for the main engine bearings. Some crankcases were designed so that the crankshaft and the main bearings are mounted and secured completely within the crankcase.

Since lubrication is essential for proper engine operation, a reservoir for collecting and holding the engine's lubricating oil is a necessary part of the engine structure. The reservoir may be called a *sump* or an *oil pan*, depending upon its design, and is usually attached directly to the engine. However, in some engines, the oil reservoir may be located at some point relatively remote from the engine; such engines may be referred to as dry sump engines.

In an engine's base, the oil sump is an integral part of the base or crankcase, which has functions other than just being an oil reservoir. Many of the smaller engines do not have a separate base or crankcase; instead, they have an oil pan, which is secured directly to the bottom of the block. In most cases, an oil pan serves only as the lower portion of the crankshaft housing and as the oil reservoir.

Some engines have flat steel plates attached to each end of the cylinder block. *End plates* add rigidity to the block and provide a surface to which may be bolted housings for such parts as gears, blowers, pumps, and generators.

Many engines, especially the larger ones, have access openings in some part of the engine frame. These openings permit access to the cylinder liners, main and connecting rod bearings, injector control shafts, and various other internal engine parts. *Access doors* (sometimes called *covers* or *plates*) for the openings are usually secured with hand wheel or nut-operated clamps and are fitted with gaskets to keep dirt and foreign material out of the engine's interior.

The *cylinder assembly* completes the structural framework of an engine. As one of the main stationary parts of an engine, the cylinder assembly, along with various related working parts, serves to confine and release the gases. For the purpose of this discussion, the cylinder assembly will be considered as consisting of the head, the liner, the studs, and the gasket.

The design of the parts of the cylinder assembly varies considerably from one type of engine to another. However, regardless of differences in design, the basic components of all cylinder assemblies function, along with related moving parts, to provide a gas- and liquid-tight space.

The barrel or bore in which an engine piston moves back and forth may be an integral part of the cylinder block or it may be a separate sleeve or liner. The first type, common in gasoline engines, has the disadvantage of not being replaceable. Practically all diesel engines are constructed with replaceable cylinder liners.

Six cylinder liners of the replaceable type illustrate some of the differences in the design of liners and the relative size of the engines represented.

The liners or bores of an internal combustion engine must be sealed tightly to form the combustion chambers. In most Navy engines (except for engines of the opposed-piston type), the space at the combustion end of a cylinder is formed and sealed by a *cylinder head* which is a separate unit from the block.

A number of engine parts, which are essential to engine operation, may be found in or attached to the cylinder head. The cylinder head may house intake and exhaust valves, valve guides and valve seats, or only exhaust valves and related parts. Rocker arm assemblies are frequently attached to the cylinder head. The fuel injection valve is almost universally in the cylinder head or heads of a diesel engine, while the spark plugs are always in the cylinder head of gasoline engines. Cylinder heads of a diesel engine may also be fitted with air starting valves, indicator and blow down valves, and safety valves.

The number of cylinder heads found on engines varies considerably. Small engines of the in-line cylinder arrangement utilize one head for all cylinders. A single head serves for all cylinders in each bank of some V-type engines. Large diesel engines generally have one cylinder head for each cylinder. Some engines use one head for each pair of cylinders.

In most cases, the seal between the cylinder head and the block depends principally upon the studs and gaskets. The studs, or stud bolts, secure the cylinder head to the cylinder block. A gasket between the head and the block is compressed to form a seal when the head is properly tightened down. In some cases, gaskets are not used between the cylinder head and block; the mating surfaces of the head and block are accurately machined to form a seal between the two parts.

Principal Moving Parts

In order that the power developed by combustion can be converted to mechanical energy, it is necessary for reciprocating motion to be changed to rotating motion. The moving parts included in the conversion process, from combustion to energy output, may be divided into the following three major groups: (1) the parts which have only reciprocating motion (pistons), (2) the parts which have both reciprocating and rotating motion (connecting rods), and (3) the parts which have only rotating motion (crankshafts and camshafts).

The first two major groups of moving parts may be further grouped under the single heading of *piston* and *rod assemblies.* Such an assembly may include a piston, piston rings, piston pin, connecting rod, and related bearings.

As one of the principal parts in the power transmitting assembly, the *piston* must be so designed and must be made of such materials that it can withstand the extreme heat and pressure of combustion. Pistons must also be light enough to keep inertia loads on related parts to a minimum. The piston aids in the sealing of the cylinder to prevent the escape of gas and transmits some of the heat through the piston rings to the cylinder wall. In addition to serving as the unit which transmits the force of combustion to the connecting rod and conducts the heat of combustion to the cylinder wall, a piston serves as a valve in opening and closing the ports of a two-stroke cycle engine. The nomenclatures for the ten parts of a typical trunk type piston are:

- Crown
- Compression Ring Grooves and Lands
- Cooling Oil Chamber
- Cooling Fins and Ribs
- Piston Pin
- BOSS
- Piston-Hub Bushing
- Skirt
- Oil Ring Grooves and Lands
- Oil Drains

Piston rings are particularly vital to engine operation in that they must effectively perform three functions: seal the cylinder, distribute and control lubricating oil on the cylinder wall, and transfer heat from the piston to the cylinder wall. All rings on a piston perform the latter function, but two general types of rings—compression and oil—are required to perform the first two functions. There are numerous types of rings in each of these groups, constructed in different ways for particular purposes.

In trunk-type piston assemblies, the connection between the piston and the connecting rod is usually the *piston pin* (sometimes referred to as the *wrist pin*) and its bearings. These parts must be of especially strong construction because the power developed in the cylinder is transmitted from the piston through the pin to the connecting rod. The pin is the pivot point where the straight-line or reciprocating motion of the piston changes to the reciprocating and rotating motion of the connecting rod. Thus, the principal forces to which a pin is subjected are the forces created by combustion and the side thrust created by the change in direction of motion.

The connecting link between the piston and crankshaft or the crankshaft and the crosshead of an engine is the *connecting rod*. In order that the forces created by combustion can be transmitted to the crankshaft, the rod changes the reciprocating motion of the piston to the rotating motion of the crankshaft.

During 1955 through 1990, most marine engines in Navy service use the trunk-type piston connected directly to the connecting rod.

The *camshaft* is a shaft with eccentric projection, called cams, designed to control the operation of valves, usually through various intermediate parts as described later in this chapter. Originally, cams were made as separate pieces and fastened to the camshaft. However, in most modern engines the cams are forged or cast as an integral part of the camshaft.

To reduce wear and to help them withstand the shock action to which they are subjected, camshafts are made of low-carbon alloy steel with the cam and journal surfaces carburized before the final grinding is done.

The *cams* are arranged on the shaft to provide the proper firing order of the cylinders served. The shape of the cam determines the point of opening and closing, the speed of opening and closing, and the amount of the valve lift. If one cylinder is properly time, the remaining cylinders are automatically in time. All cylinders will be affected if there is a change in timing.

The *camshaft* is driven by the *crankshaft* by various means, the most common being by gears or by a chain and sprocket. The camshaft for a 4-stroke cycle engine must turn at one- half of the crankshaft speed; while in the 2-stroke cycle engine, it turns at the same speed as the crankshaft.

The location of the crankshaft in various engines differs. Camshaft location depends on the arrangement of the valve mechanism.

One of the principal engine parts which has only rotating motion is the *crankshaft*. As one of the largest and most important moving parts in an engine, the crankshaft changes the movement of the piston and the connecting rod into the rotating motion required to drive such items as reduction gears, propeller shafts, generators, pumps, etc. Because of its function, the crankshaft is subjected to all the forces developed in an engine.

While crankshafts of a few larger engines are of the built-up type (forged in separate sections and flanged together), the crankshafts of most modern engines are of the one-piece type construction. The parts of a crankshaft may be identified by various terms; however, the technical manuals had to be referred to for most of the engines used by the Navy.

The speed of rotation of the crankshaft increases each time the shaft receives a power impulse from one of the pistons; and it then gradually decreases until another power impulse is received. These fluctuations in speed (their number depending upon the number of cylinders firing in one crankshaft revolution) would result in an undesirable situation with respect to the driven mechanism as well as the engine; therefore, some means must be provided to stabilize shaft rotation. In some engines, this is accomplished by installing a *flywheel* on the crankshaft; in others, the motion of such engine parts as the crankpins, webs, lower ends of connecting rods, and such driven units as the clutch, generator, etc., serve the purpose. The need for a flywheel decreases as the number of cylinders firing in one revolution of the crankshaft and the mass of the moving parts attached to the crankshaft increases.

A flywheel stores up energy during the power event and releases it during the remaining events of the operating cycle. In other words, when the speed of the shaft tends to increase, the flywheel absorbs energy, and when the speed tends to decrease, the flywheel gives up energy to the shaft in an effort to keep shaft rotation uniform. In doing this, a flywheel (1) keeps variations in speed within desired limits at all loads; (2) limits the increase or decrease in speed during sudden changes of load; (3) aids in forcing the piston through the compression event when an engine is running at low or idling speed; and (4) helps bring the engine up to speed when it is being cranked.

An important group of engine parts consists of the bearings. Some bearings remain stationary in performing their function while others move. One principal group of stationary bearings in an engine is that which supports the crankshaft. These bearings are generally called main engine bearings. Main bearings in most engines were of the sliding contact, or plain type, consisting of two halves or shells.

Main bearings are subjected to a fluctuating load. This is also true of the crankpin bearings and the piston-pin bearings. However, the manner in which main journal bearings are loaded depends upon the type of engine in which they are used.

In a 2-stroke cycle engine, a load is always placed on the lower half of the main bearings and the lower half of the piston pin bearings in the connecting rod; meanwhile the load is placed upon the upper half of the connecting rod bearings at the crankshaft end of the rod. This is true because the forces of combustion are greater than the inertia forces created by the moving parts.

In a 4-stroke cycle engine, the load is applied first on one bearing shell and then on the other. The reversal of pressure is the result of the large forces of inertia imposed during the intake and exhaust strokes. In other words, inertia tends to lift the crankshaft in its bearings during the intake and exhaust strokes.

There is a definite reversal of load application on the main bearings of a double-acting engine. In this case, the reversal is caused by combustion taking place first on one end of the piston and then on the other.

The bearings used in connection with piston pins are of three types: the integral bearing, the sleeve bearing or bushing, and the needle type roller bearing. The bearings in the bosses (hubs) of most pistons are of the sleeve bushing type. However, in a few cases, the boss bearings are an integral part of the piston. In such cases, the bearing surface is precision bored directly in the bosses. Pistons fitted with stationary piston pins require no bearing surfaces in the bosses.

Even though the piston pins in most engines are equipped with bushing type bearings, some have been fitted with bearings of the needle roller type.

The types of bearings used for main bearings and in connection with piston-pin assemblies are representative of those used at other points in an engine where bearing surfaces are required.

Not all of the parts that make a complete engine have been covered in the preceding section of this chapter. Since many engine parts and accessories are commonly associated with the *systems of an engine*, functions of some of the principal components not covered to this point are considered with the applicable system that they affect.

Engine Air Systems

Parts and accessories which supply the cylinders of an engine with air for combustion, and remove the waste gases after combustion and the power events are finished, are commonly referred to as the *intake and exhaust systems*. These systems are closely related and, in some cases, are referred to as the air systems of an engine.

The following information on air systems deals primarily with the systems of diesel engines; nevertheless, much of the information dealing with the parts of diesel engine air systems is also applicable to most of the parts in similar systems of gasoline engines. However, the intake event in the cycle of operation of a gasoline engine includes the admission of air and fuel as a mixture to the cylinder. For this reason, the intake system of a gasoline engine differs, in some respects, from that of a diesel engine. (See subsequent section on fuel systems).

A discussion of the air systems of diesel engines frequently involves the use of two terms which identify processes related to the functions of the intake and exhaust systems. The terms: *scavenging* and *supercharging*—and the processes they identify are common to many of the then modern diesel engines.

In the intake systems of all modern 2-stroke cycle engines and some 4-stroke cycle engines, a device, usually a blower is installed to increase the flow of air into the cylinders. This is accomplished by the blower compressing the air and forcing it into an air box or manifold (reservoir) which surrounds or is attached to the cylinders of an engine. An increased amount of air under constant pressure is available as required during the cycle of operation.

The increased amount of air available because of blower action is used to fill the cylinder with a fresh charge of air and, during the process, aids in clearing the cylinder of the gases of combustion. This process is called *scavenging*. The intake system of some engines, especially those operating on the 2-stroke cycle, is sometimes called the *scavenging system*. The air forced into the cylinder is called *scavenge* (or *scavenging*) air and the ports through which it enters are called *scavenge ports*.

The process of scavenging must be accomplished in a relatively short portion of the operating cycle; however, the duration of the process differs in 2- and 4-stroke cycle engines. In a 2-stroke cycle engine, the process takes place during the later part of the downstroke (expansion) and the early part of the upstroke (compression). In a 4-stroke cycle engine, scavenging takes place when the piston is nearing and passing TDC during the latter part of an upstroke (exhaust and the early part of a downstroke (intake). The intake and exhaust openings are both open during this interval of time. The overlap of intake and exhaust permits the air from the blower to pass through the cylinder into the exhaust manifold, cleaning out the exhaust gases from the cylinder and, at the same time, cooling the hot engine parts.

Scavenging air must be so directed, when it enters the cylinder of an engine, that the waste gases be removed from the remote parts of the cylinder. The two principal methods by which this is accomplished are sometimes referred to as *port* scavenging and *valve* scavenging. Port scavenging may be of the direct (or cross-flow) loop (or return), or uniflow type.

An increase in air flow into cylinders of an engine can be used to increase power output, in addition to being used for scavenging. Since the burning of fuel develops the power of an engine, an increase of power requires more fuel; the increased fuel, in turn, requires more air, since each pound of fuel requires a certain amount of air for combustion. Supplying more air to the combustion spaces that can be supplied through the action of atmospheric pressure and piston action (in 4-stroke cycle engines) or scavenging air (in 2-stroke cycle engines) is called *supercharging*.

In some 2-stroke cycle diesel engines, the cylinders are supercharged during the air intake simply by increasing the amount and pressure of scavenge air. The same blower is used for supercharging and scavenging. Whereas scavenging is accomplished by admitting air under low-pressure into the cylinder while the exhaust valves or ports are open, supercharging is done with the exhaust ports or valves closed. This latter arrangement enables the blower to force air under pressure into the cylinder and thereby increase the amount of air available for combustion. The increase in pressure resulting from the compressing action of the blower will depend upon the engine involved, but it is usually low, ranging from 1 to 5 psi. With this increase in pressure, and the amount of air available for combustion, there is a corresponding increase in the air-fuel ratio and in combustion efficiency within the cylinder. In other words, a given size engine which is supercharged can develop more power than the same size engine which is not supercharged.

Supercharging a 4-stroke cycle diesel engine requires the addition of a blower to the intake system since the operations of exhaust and intake in an unsupercharged engine are performed by the action of the piston. The timing of the valves in a supercharged 4-stroke cycle engine is also different from that in a similar engine that is not supercharged. In the supercharged engine the intake-valve opening is advanced and the exhaust-valve closing is retarded so that there is considerable overlap of the intake and exhaust events. This overlap increases power, the amount of the increase depending upon the supercharging pressure. The increased overlap of the valve openings in a supercharged 4-stroke cycle engine also permits the air pressure created by the blower to be used in removing gases from the cylinder during the exhaust event. How the opening and the closing of the intake and exhaust valves or ports affect both scavenging and supercharging, and the differences in these processes as they occurred in supercharged 2- and 4-stroke cycle engines, were seen by studying their diagrams.

When these diagrams were being studied, it was kept in mind that the crankshaft of a 4-stroke cycle engine made two complete revolutions in one cycle of operation while the shaft in a 2-stroke cycle engine made only one revolution per cycle. It should also be remembered that the exhaust and intake events in a 2-stroke cycle engine did not involve complete piston strokes as they did in a 4-stroke cycle engine.

Even though the primary purpose of a diesel engine *intake system* is to supply the air required for combustion, the system generally had to perform one or more additional functions. In most cases, the system cleaned the air and reduced the noise created by the air as it entered the engine. In order to accomplish the functions of intake, an intake system may include an air silencer, an air cleaner and screen, an air box or header, intake valves or ports, a blower, an air heater, and an air cooler. Not all of these parts were common to every intake system.

The system that functions primarily to convey gases away from the cylinders of an engine is called the *exhaust system*. In addition to this principal function, an exhaust system may be designed to perform one or more of the following functions: muffle exhaust noise, quench sparks, remove solid material from exhaust gases, and furnish energy to a turbine-driven supercharger.

Operating Mechanics for System Parts and Accessories

To this point, consideration has been given only to the main engine parts—stationary and moving—and to two of the systems common to internal combustion engines. At various points in this chapter, reference has been made to the operation of some of the engine parts. For example, it has been pointed out that the valves open and close at the proper time in the operating cycle and that the impellers or lobes of a blower rotate to compress intake air. However, little consideration has been given to the source of power or to the mechanisms that cause these parts to operate.

In many cases, the mechanism, which transmits power for the operation of the engine valves and blower, may also transmit power to parts and accessories that are components of various engine systems. For example, such items as the governor; fuel, lubricating, and water pumps; and overspeed trips, are, in some engines, operated by the same mechanism. Since mechanisms that transmit power to operate specific parts and accessories may be related to more than one engine system, such operating mechanisms are considered here before the remaining engine systems are discussed.

The parts that make up the operating mechanisms of an engine may be divided into two groups: the group that forms the drive mechanisms and the group that forms the *actuating mechanisms.* The source of power for the operating mechanisms of an engine is the crankshaft.

As used in this chapter, the term drive mechanism identifies the group of parts that takes power from the crankshaft and transmits that power to various engine parts and accessories. In engines, the drive mechanisms does not change the type of motion, but it may change the direction of motion. For example, the impellers or lobes of a blower are driven or operated as a result of rotary motion which is taken from the crankshaft and transmitted to the impellers or lobes by the drive mechanism, an arrangement of gears and shafts. While the type of motion (rotary) remains the same, the direction of motion of one impeller or lobe is opposite to that of the other impeller or lobe because of the gear arrangements within the drive mechanism.

A drive mechanism may be of the gear, chain or belt type. Of these, the gear type is the most common; however, some engines are equipped with chain assemblies, A combination of gears and chains is used as the driving mechanism in some engines.

Some engines have a single drive mechanism, which transmits power for the operation of engine parts and accessories. In other cases, there may be two or more separate mechanisms. When separate assemblies are used, the one, which transmits power for the operation of the accessories, is called the accessory drive. Some engines have more than one *accessory drive.* A separate drive mechanism, which is used to transmit power for the operation of engine valves, is generally called the *camshaft* drive or *timing mechanism.*

The camshaft drive, as the name implies, transmits power to the camshaft of the engine. The shaft, in turn, transmits the power through a combination of parts, which causes the engine valves to operate. Since the valves of an engine must open and close at the proper moment (with respect to the position of the piston) and remain in the open and closed positions for definite periods, a fixed relationship must be maintained between the rotational speeds of the crankshaft and the camshaft. Camshaft drives are designed to maintain the proper relationship between the speeds of the two shafts. In maintaining this relationship, the drive causes the camshaft to rotate at crankshaft speed in a 2-stroke cycle engine; and at one-half crankshaft speed in a 4-stroke cycle engine.

The term actuating mechanism, identifies that combination of parts which receives power from the drive mechanism and transmits the power to the engine valves. In order for the valves (intake, exhaust, fuel injection, air starter) to operate, there must be a change in the type of motion. In other words, the rotary motion of the crankshaft and drive mechanism must be changed to a reciprocating motion. The group of parts, which, by changing the type of motion, causes the valves of an engine to operate, is generally referred to as the *valve actuating mechanism*. A valve-actuating mechanism may include the cams, cam followers, push rods, rocker arms, and valve springs. In some engines, the camshaft is so located that the need for push rods is eliminated. In such cases, the cam follower is a part of the rocker arm. (Some actuating mechanisms are designed to transform reciprocating motion into rotary motion, but in internal combustion engines, most actuating mechanisms change rotary motion into reciprocating motion).

There is considerable variation in the design and arrangement of the parts of operating mechanisms found in different engines. The size of an engine, the cycle of operation, the cylinder arrangement, and other factors govern the design and arrangement of the components as well as the design and arrangement of the mechanisms.

The mechanisms, which supply power for the operation of the valves and accessories of gasoline engines, are basically the same as those found in diesel engines. Some manufacturers utilize mechanisms consisting primarily of chain assemblies, while others use gears as the primary means of transmitting power to engine parts. Combination gear-chain drive assemblies are used on some gasoline engines.

Engine Fuel Systems

The method of getting fuel into the cylinder is one of the major differences between gasoline and diesel engines. As pointed out earlier, fuel for gasoline engines is mixed with air outside the cylinder and the mixture is then drawn into the cylinder and compressed. On the other hand, fuel for diesel engines is injected or sprayed into the combustion space after the air is already compressed. The equipment, which supplies fuel to the cylinders of a gasoline engine, would necessarily be different from that of a diesel engine.

There are several types of *fuel injection systems* in use. However, the function of each type is the same. The primary function of a fuel injection system is to deliver fuel to the cylinders, under specified conditions. The conditions must be in accordance with the power requirements of the engine.

The first condition to be met is that of the injection equipment. The quantity of fuel injected determines the amount of energy available, through combustion, to the engine. Smooth engine operation and even distribution of the load between the cylinders depend upon the same volume of fuel being admitted to a particular cylinder each time it fires, and upon equal volumes of fuel being delivered to all cylinders of the engine. The measuring device of a fuel injection system must also be designed to vary the amount of fuel being delivered as changes in load and speed vary.

In addition to measuring the amount of fuel injected, the system must properly time injection to ensure efficient combustion, so maximum energy can be obtained from the fuel. Early injection tends to develop excessive cylinder pressures; and extremely early injection will cause knocking. Late injection tends to decrease power output; and, if extremely late, it will cause incomplete combustion. In many engines, fuel injection equipment is designed to vary the time of injection, as speed or load varies.

A fuel system must also control the rate of injection. The rate at which fuel is injected determines the rate of combustion. The rate of injection at the start should be low enough that excessive fuel does not accumulate in the cylinder during the initial ignition delay (before combustion begins). Injection should proceed at such a rate that the rise in combustion pressure is not excessive, yet the rate of injection must be such that fuel is introduced as rapidly as is permissible in order to obtain complete combustion. An incorrect rate of injection will affect engine operation in the same way as improper timing. If the rate of injection is too high, the results will be similar to those caused by an excessively early injection; if the rate is too low, the results will be similar to those caused by an excessively late injection.

A fuel injection system must increase the pressure of the fuel sufficiently to overcome compression pressures and to ensure proper distribution of the fuel injected into the combustion space. Proper distribution is essential if the fuel is to mix thoroughly with the air and burn efficiently. While pressure is a prime contributing factor, the distribution of the fuel is influenced in part, by "atomization" and "penetration" of the fuel. As used in connection with fuel injection, atomization means the breaking up of the fuel, as it enters the cylinder, into small particles, which form a mist-like spray. Penetration is the distance through which the fuel particles are carried by the kinetic energy imparted to them as they leave the injector or nozzle.

Atomization is obtained when the liquid fuel, under high-pressure, passes through the small opening or openings in the injector or nozzle. As the fuel enters the combustion space, high velocity is developed because the pressure in the cylinder is lower than the fuel pressure. The friction created as the fuel passes through the air at high velocity causes the fuel to break up into small particles. Penetration of the fuel particles depends chiefly upon the viscosity of the fuel, the fuel-injection pressure, and the size of the opening through which the fuel enters the cylinder.

Fuel must be atomized into particles sufficiently small so as to produce a satisfactory ignition delay period. However, if the atomization process reduces the size of the fuel particles too much, they will lack penetration; the smaller the particles the less the penetration. Lack of sufficient penetration results in the small particles of fuel igniting before they have been properly distributed. Since penetration and atomization tend to oppose each other, a compromise in the degree of each is necessary in the design of fuel injection equipment if uniform fuel distribution is to be obtained. The pressure required for efficient injection, and, in turn, proper distribution, is dependent upon the compression pressure in the cylinder, the size of the opening through which the fuel enters the combustion space, the shape of the combustion space, and the amount of turbulence created in the combustion space.

The fuel system of a gasoline engine is basically similar to that of a diesel engine, except that a *carburetor* is used instead of injection equipment. While injection equipment handles fuel only, the carburetor handles both air and fuel. The carburetor must meet requirements similar to those of an injection system except that in the carburetor air is also involved. In brief, the carburetor must accurately meter fuel and air, and in varying percentages, according to engine requirements. The carburetor also functions to vaporize the fuel charge and then mix it with the air, in the proper ratio.

The amount of fuel mixed with the air must be carefully regulated, and must change with the engine's different speeds and loads. The amount of fuel required by an engine, which is warming-up, is different from the amount required by an engine that has reached operating temperature. Special fuel adjustment is needed for rapid acceleration. The modern carburetor meets all of these varying requirements automatically.

Engine Ignition Systems

The methods by which the fuel mixture is ignited in the cylinders of diesel and gasoline engines differ as much as the methods of obtaining a combustible mixture in the cylinders of the two engines. An ignition system, as such, is not commonly associated with diesel engines. There is no one group of parts in a diesel engine that functions only to cause ignition, as there is in a gasoline engine. However, a diesel engine does have an "ignition system;" otherwise, combustion would not take place in the cylinders.

In a diesel engine, the parts that may be considered as forming the ignition system are the piston, the cylinder liner, and the cylinder head. These parts are not commonly thought of as forming an ignition system since they are generally associated with other functions such as forming the combustion space and transmitting power. Nevertheless, ignition in a diesel engine depends upon the piston, the cylinder, and the head. These parts not only form the space where combustion takes place but also provide the means by which the air is compressed to generate the heat necessary for self-ignition of the combustible mixture. In other words, both the source (air) of ignition heat and its generation (compression) are wholly within a diesel engine.

This is not true of a gasoline engine because the combustion cycles of the two types of engines are different. In a gasoline engine, even though the piston, the cylinder, and the head form the combustion space, as in a diesel engine, the heat necessary for ignition is caused by energy from a source external to the combustion space. The completion of the ignition process, involving the transformation of mechanical energy into electrical energy and then into heat energy, requires several parts, each performing a specific function. The parts which make the transformation of energy and the system which they form are commonly thought of when reference is made to an ignition system.

The spark that causes the ignition of the explosive mixture in the cylinders of a gasoline engine is produced when electricity is forced across a gap formed by two electrodes in the combustion chamber. The electrical ignition system furnishes the spark periodically to each cylinder, at a predetermined position of piston travel. In order to accomplish this function, an electrical ignition system must have, first of all, either a source of electrical energy or a means of developing electrical energy. In some cases, a storage battery is used as the source of energy; in other cases, a magneto generates electricity for the ignition system. The voltage from either a battery or a magneto is not sufficiently high enough to overcome the resistance created by pressure in the combustion chamber and to cause the proper spark in the gap formed by the two electrodes in the combustive chamber. Therefore, it is essential that an ignition system include a device, which increases the voltage of the electricity supplied to the system sufficiently to cause a "hot" spark in the gap of the spark plug. The device, which performs this function, is generally called an ignition coil or induction coil.

Since a spark must occur shortly in each cylinder at a specific time, an ignition system must include a device that controls the timing of the flow of electricity to each cylinder. This control is accomplished by interrupting the flow of electricity from the source to the voltage-increasing device (ignition coil). The interruption of the flow of electricity also plays an important part in the process of increasing voltage. The interrupting device is generally called the breaker assembly. A device that will distribute electricity to the different cylinders in the proper firing order is also necessary. The part that performs this function is called the distributing mechanism. Spark plugs to provide the gaps and wiring and switches to connect the parts of the system are essential to complete an ignition system.

All ignition systems are basically the same, except for the source of electrical energy. The source of energy is frequently used as a basis for classifying ignition systems; thus the battery-ignition system and the magneto-ignition system.

Engine Cooling Systems

A great amount of heat is generated within an engine during operation. Combustion produces the greater portion of this heat; however, compression of gases within the cylinders and friction between moving parts add to the total amount of heat developed within an engine. Since the temperature of combustion alone is about twice that at which iron melts, it is apparent that, without some means of dissipating heat, an engine would operate for only a very limited time. Without proper temperature control, the lubricating-oil film between moving parts would be destroyed, proper clearance between parts could not be maintained, and metals would tend to fail.

Of the total heat supplied to the cylinder of an engine by the burning fuel, only one-third, approximately, is transformed into useful work; an equal amount is lost to the exhaust gases. This leaves approximately 30 to 35 percent of the heat of combustion which must be removed in order to prevent damage to engine parts. The greater portion of the heat that may produce harmful results is transferred from the engine through the medium of water; lubricating oil, air, and fuel are also utilized to aid in the cooling of an engine. All methods of heat transfer are utilized in keeping engine parts and fluids (air, water, fuel, and lubricating oil) at safe operating temperatures.

In a marine engine, the cooling system may be of the open or closed type. In the open system, the engine is cooled directly by saltwater.

In the closed system, fresh water (or an anti-freeze solution) is circulated through the engine. The fresh water is then cooled by salt water. In marine installations, the closed system is the type commonly used; however, some older marine installations use a system of the open type. The cooling systems of diesel and gasoline engines are similar mechanically and in function performed.

The cooling system of an engine may include such parts as pumps, coolers, engine passages, water manifolds, valves, expansion tank, piping, strainers, connections, and instruments.

Even though there are many types and models of engines used by the Navy, the cooling systems of most of these engines included the same basic parts. However, design and location of parts differed considerably from one engine to another.

Engine Lubricating Systems

It is essential to the operation of an engine that the contacting surfaces of all moving parts of an engine be kept free from abrasion and that there be a minimum of friction and wear. If sliding contact is made by two dry metal surfaces under pressure, excessive friction, heat, and wear result. Friction, heat, and wear can be greatly reduced if metal-to-metal contact is prevented by keeping a clean film of lubricant between the metal surfaces.

Lubrication and the system which supplies lubricating oil to engine parts that involve sliding or rolling contact are as important to successful engine operation as air, fuel, and heat are to combustion. It is important not only that the proper type of lubricant be used, but also that the lubricant be supplied to the engine parts in the proper quantities, at the proper temperature, and that provisions be made to remove any impurities which enter the system. The engine lubricating oil system is designed to fulfill the above requirements.

The lubricating system of an engine may be thought of as consisting of two main divisions, that external to the engine and that within the engine. The internal division, or engine part, of the system consists principally of passages and piping; the external part of the system includes several components that aid in supplying the oil in the proper quantity, at the proper temperature, and free of impurities. In order to meet these requirements, the lubricating systems of many engines include, external to the engine, such parts as tanks and sumps, pumps, coolers, strainers and filters, and purifiers.

The engine system, which supplies the oil required to perform the functions of lubrication, is of the pressure type in practically all modern internal combustion engines. Even though many variations exist in the details of engine lubricating systems, the parts of such a system and its operation are basically the same, whether the system is in a diesel or a gasoline engine. Any variance between the systems of the two types of engines is generally due to differences in engine design and in opinions of manufacturers as to the best location of the component parts of the system. In many cases, similar types of components are used in the systems of diesel and gasoline engines.

TRANSMISSION OF ENGINE POWER

The fundamental characteristics of an internal combustion engine make it necessary, in many cases, for the drive mechanism to change both the speed and the direction of shaft rotation in the driven mechanism. There are various methods by which required changes of speed and directions may be made during the transmission of power from the driving unit to the driven unit. In most installations, the job is accomplished by a drive mechanism consisting principally of gears and shafts.

The process of transmitting engine power to a point where it can be used in performing useful work involves a number of factors. Two of these factors are torque and speed.

The force, which tends to cause a rotational movement of an object, is called *torque* or "twist." The crankshaft of an engine supplies a twisting force to the gears and shafts that transmit power to the driven unit. Gears are used to increase or decrease torque. If the right combination of gears is installed between the engine and the driven unit, the torque or "twist" will be sufficient to operate the driven unit.

If maximum efficiency is to be obtained, an engine must operate at a certain speed. In order to obtain efficient engine operation, it might be necessary in some installations for the engine to operate at a higher speed than that required for efficient operation of the driven unit. In other cases, the speed of the engine may have to be lower than the speed of the driven unit. Through a combination of gears, the speed of the driven unit can be increased or decreased so that the proper speed ratio exists between the units.

Types of Drive Mechanisms

The term *indirect drive* describes a drive mechanism that changes speed and torque. Drives of this type are common to many marine engine installations. Where the speed and the torque of an engine need not be changed in order to drive a machine satisfactorily, the mechanism used is a *direct drive*. Drives of this type are commonly used where the engine furnishes power for the operation of auxiliaries such as generators and pumps.

Indirect Drives

The drive mechanism of most engine-powered ships and many boats are of the indirect type. With indirect drive, the power developed by the engine(s) is transmitted to the propeller(s) indirectly, through an intermediate mechanism, which reduces the shaft speed. Speed reduction may be accomplished mechanically (by a combination of gears) or by electrical means.

Mechanical drives include devices which reduce the shaft speed of the driven unit, provide a means for reversing the direction of shaft rotation in the driven unit, and permit quick-disconnect of the driving unit from the driven unit.

The combination of gears, which effects the speed reduction, is called a reduction gear. In most diesel engine installations, the reduction ratio does not exceed 3 to 1; there are some units, however, which have reductions as high as 6 to 1.

The propelling equipment of a boat or a ship must be capable of providing backing-down power as well as forward motive power. There are a few ships and boats in which backing down is accomplished by reversing the pitch of the propeller; in most ships, however, backing down is accomplished by reversing the direction of rotation of the propeller shaft. In mechanical drives, reversing the direction of rotation of the propeller shaft may be accomplished in one of two ways: by reversing the direction of engine rotation, or by the use of reverse gears. Of these two methods, the use of reverse gears is more commonly employed in modern installations.

More than reducing speed and reversing the direction of shaft rotation is required of the drive mechanism of a ship or a boat. It is frequently necessary to allow an engine to operate without power being transmitted to the propeller. For this reason, the drive mechanism of a ship or boat must include a means of disconnecting the engine from the propeller shaft. Devices used for this purpose are called *clutches* and *couplings*.

The arrangement of the components in an indirect drive varies, depending upon the type and size of the installation. In some small installations, the clutch or coupling, the reverse gear, and the reduction gear may be combined in a single unit; in other installations, the clutch or coupling and the reverse gear may be in one housing and the reduction gear in a separate housing attached to the reverse-gear housing. Drive mechanisms arranged in either manner are usually called *transmissions*.

In one particular transmission, the bearing carrier divides the housing into two sections. The clutch or coupling assembly is in the forward section, and the gear assembly is in the after section of the housing. In another transmission, the clutch assembly and the reverse gear assembly are in one housing, while the reduction gear unit is in a separate housing (attached to the clutch and the reverse gear housing).

In large engine installations, the clutch or coupling and the reverse gear may be combined; or they may be separate units, located between the engine and a separate reduction gear; or the clutch or coupling may be separate and the reverse gear and the reduction gear may be combined.

In most geared-drive, multiple-propeller ships, the propulsion units are independent of each other.

In some installations, the drive mechanism is arranged so that two or more engines drive a single propeller. This is accomplished by having the driving gear which is on, or connected to, the crankshaft of each engine transmit power to the driven gear on the propeller shaft. In one type of installation, each of two propellers is driven by four diesel engines.

The drive mechanism illustrated includes four clutch assemblies (one mounted to each engine flywheel) and one gear box. The box contains two drive pinions and the main drive gear. Each pinion is driven by the clutch or coupling shafts of two engines, through splines in the pinion hubs. The pinions drive the single main gear, which is connected to the propeller shaft.

Electric drives are used in the propulsion plants of some diesel-driven ships. With electric drive, there is no mechanical connection between the engine(s) and the propeller(s). In such plants, the diesel engines are connected directly to generators. The electricity produced by such an engine-driven generator is transmitted, through cables, to a motor. The motor is connected to the propeller shaft directly or indirectly through a reduction gear. When a reduction gear is included in a diesel-electric drive, the gear is located between the motor and the propeller.

The generator and the motor of a diesel-electric drive may be of the alternating current (AC) type or of the direct current (DC) type; almost all diesel-electric drives in the Navy, however, are of the direct current type. Since the speed of a d-c motor varies directly with the voltage furnished by the generator, the control system of an electric drive is so arranged that the generator voltage can be changed at any time. An increase or decrease in generator voltage is used as a means of controlling the speed of the propeller. Changes in generator voltage may be brought about by electrical means, by changes in engine speed, and by a combination of these methods. The controls of an electric drive may be in a location remote from the engine, such as the pilot house.

In an electric drive, reversing the direction of rotation of the propeller is not accomplished by the use of a reverse gear. The electrical system is arranged so that the flow of current through the motor can be reversed. This reversal of current flow causes the motor to revolve in the opposite direction. Thus, the direction of rotation of the motor and of the propeller can be controlled by manipulating the electrical controls.

Direct Drives

In some marine engine installations, power from the engine is transmitted to the driven unit without a change in shaft speed; that is, by a direct drive. In a direct drive, the connection between the engine and the driven unit may consist of a "solid" coupling, a flexible coupling, or a combination of both. A clutch may or may not be included in a direct drive, depending upon the type of installation. In some installations, a reverse gear is included.

Solid couplings vary considerably in design. Some solid couplings consist of two flanges bolted solidly together. In other direct drives, the driven unit is attached directly to the engine crankshaft by a nut.

Solid couplings offer a positive means of transmitting torque from the crankshaft of an engine; however, a solid connection does not allow for any misalignment nor does it absorb any of the torsional vibrations transmitted from the engine crankshaft or shaft vibrations.

Since solid coupling will not absorb vibration and will not permit any misalignment, most direct drives consist of a flange-type coupling which is used in connection with a flexible coupling. Connections of the flexible type are common to the drives of many auxiliaries, such as engine-generator sets. Flexible couplings are also used in indirect drives to connect the engine to the drive mechanism.

The two solid halves of a flexible coupling are joined by a flexible element. The flexible element is made of rubber, neoprene, or steel springs.

If the coupling has radial spring packs as the flexible element, the power from the engine is transmitted from the inner ring, or spring holder, of the coupling, through a number of spring packs to the outer spring holder, or driven member. A large driving disk connects the outer spring holder to the flange on the driven shaft. The pilot on the end of the crankshaft fits into a bronze, bushed bearing on the outer driving disk to center the driven shaft. The ring gear of the jacking mechanism is pressed onto the rim of the outer spring holder.

The inner driving disk, through which the camshaft gear train is driven, is fastened to the outer spring holder. A splined ring gear is bolted to the inner driving disk. This helical, internal gear fits on the outer part of the crankshaft gear and forms an elastic drive, through the crankshaft gear which rides on the crankshaft. The splined ring gear is split and the two parts are bolted together with a spacer block at each split-joint.

CLUTCHES, REVERSE GEARS AND REDUCTION GEARS

Clutches may be used on direct-driven propulsion Navy engines to provide a means of disconnecting the engine from the propeller shaft. In small engines, clutches are usually combined with reverse gears and used for maneuvering the ship. In large engines, special types of clutches are used to obtain special coupling or control characteristics, and to prevent torsional vibration.

Reverse gears are used on marine engines to reverse the direction of rotation of the propeller shaft, when maneuvering the ship, without changing the direction of rotation of the engine. They are used principally on relatively small engines. If a high-output engine has a reverse gear, the gear is used for low-speed operation only, and does not have full-load and full-speed capacity. For maneuvering ships with large direct-propulsion engines, the engines are reversed.

Reduction gears are used to obtain low propeller-shaft speed with a high engine speed. When accomplishing this, the gears correlate two conflicting requirements of a marine engine installation. These opposing requirements are: (1) for minimum weight and size for a given power output, engines must have a relatively high rotative speed; and (2) for maximum efficiency, propellers must rotate at a relatively low speed, particularly where high thrust capacity is desired.

Friction Clutches and Gear Assemblies

Friction clutches are commonly used with smaller, high-speed engines, up to 500 hp. However, certain friction clutches, in combination with a jaw-type clutch, are used with engines up to 1,400 hp; and pneumatic clutches, with a cylindrical friction surface, with engines up to 2,000 hp.

Friction clutches are of two general styles; the disk and the band styles. In addition, friction clutches can be classified into dry and wet types, depending upon whether the friction surfaces operate with or without a lubricant. The designs of both types are similar, except that the wet clutches require a large friction area because of the reduced friction coefficient between the lubricated surfaces. The advantages of wet clutches are smoother operation and less wear of the friction surfaces. Wear results from slippage between the surfaces not only during engagement and disengagement, but also, to a certain extent, during the operation of the mechanism. Some wet-type clutches are filled with oil periodically; in other clutches the oil, being a part of the engine-lubricating system, is circulated continuously. Such a friction clutch incorporates provisions that will prevent worn-off particles from being carried by the circulating lubricating oil to the bearings, gears, etc.

The friction surfaces are generally constructed of different materials, one being of cast iron or steel; the other is lined with some asbestos-base composition, or sintered iron or bronze for dry clutches, and bronze, cast iron, or steel for wet clutches. Cast-iron surfaces are preferred because of their better bearing qualities and greater resistance to scoring or scuffing.

Sintered blocks are made of finely powdered iron or bronze particles, molded in forms to the desired shape, under high temperature and pressure.

As far as engagement of the friction clutches is concerned, the application of force-producing friction can be obtained either by mechanically jamming the friction surfaces together by some toggle-action linkage, or through stiff springs (coil, leaf, or flat-disk type). Air pressure is also used to engage friction clutches.

Twin-Disk Clutch and Gear Mechanism

One of the several types of transmissions used by the Navy was the twin disk transmission mechanism. Gray Marine high-speed diesel engines were generally equipped with a combination clutch, and reverse and reduction gear unit— all contained in a single housing, at the after end of the engine.

The clutch assembly of the twin disk transmission mechanism is contained in the part of the housing nearest the engine. It is a dry-type, twin-disk clutch with two driving disks. Each disk is connected, through shafting, to a separate reduction gear train in the after part of the housing. One disk and reduction train is for reverse rotation of the shaft and propeller, the other disk and reduction train for forward rotation. The forward and reverse gear trains for Gray Marine engines are different; however, the operation of the mechanisms is basically the same. Since the gears for forward and reverse rotation of the twin-disk clutch and gear mechanism remain in mesh at all times, there is no shifting of gears. In shifting the mechanism, only the floating plate, located between the forward and reverse disks is shifted. The shifting mechanism is a sliding sleeve, which does not rotate, but has a loose sliding fit around the hollow forward shaft. A throwout fork (yoke) engages a pair of shifter blocks pinned on either side of the sliding sleeve.

The clutch operating lever moves the throwout fork, which in turn shifts the sliding sleeve lengthwise along the forward shaft. When the operating lever is placed forward, the sliding sleeve is forced backward. In this position, the linkages of the spring-loaded mechanism pull the floating pressure plate against the forward disk, and cause forward rotation. When the operating lever is pulled back as far as it can go, the sliding sleeve is pushed forward. In this position, the floating pressure plate engages the reverse disk and back plate for reverse rotation.

The clutch has a positive neutral which is set by placing the operating lever in a middle position. Then the sliding sleeve is also in a middle position, and the floating plate rotates freely between the two clutch disks. (The only control that the operator had was to cause the floating plate to bear heavily against either the forward disk or the reverse disk or to put the floating plate in the positive neutral position so that it rotated freely between the two disks).

The reversing gear unit is lubricated separately from the engine by its own splash system. The oil level of the gear housing should never be kept over the high mark because too much oil will cause overheating of the gear unit. The oil is cooled by air that is blown through the baffled top cover by the rotating clutch. Grease fittings are installed for bearings not lubricated by the oil.

Joe's Double Clutch Reverse Gear

A gear mechanism found on many power boats was Joe's double clutch reverse gear. The drive from the engine crankshaft is taken into the clutch and reverse gear housing by an extension of the crankshaft drive gear. The crankshaft rotation is transmitted to the reduction gear shaft through the clutch and the reverse gear unit.

If one could open the clutch and reverse gear housing and watch the reverse gear drum and the reduction gear shaft while the engine is running, the following operation would have been observed:

When the operating lever is thrown forward, the drum and reduction gear shaft rotate in the same direction as the engine crankshaft. This causes forward rotation of the propeller.

In the intermediate position of the operating lever, the drum rotates but the reduction gear shaft remains stationary. This is the neutral setting.

Forward rotation is obtained by dual clutch action while reverse rotation is obtained through the operation of the planetary gears. The unit consists of a housing enclosing a split conical clutch and a multi-plate friction clutch and gearing. Additional components include the collar and yoke and an outer brake band with an operating toggle mechanism. Movement of the sliding collar selects the direction of rotation.

When the operating lever is placed in the forward position, the linkage between the lever and the collar and yoke assembly slides the collar lengthwise to the left along the reduction gear shaft. This motion operates the toggle assembly, which, in turn, drives the three plungers to the right, pressing them hard against the disk clutch.

When the plungers are driven hard against the disk clutch, the disks are locked together by friction. This locks the drum housing to the propeller drive sleeve. In addition, the force of the plungers on the disk clutch is transmitted to the bearing cage, which is a cylinder containing the reverse gear pinions. The bearing cage, in turn, is pressed against the cone clutch. The cone clutch is forced against its seat in the front cover of the gear box, clamping the clutch to the front cover by friction. Since the cone clutch is in mesh on its inner surface with the engine sleeve, which is in turn keyed to the engine shaft, the front cover is now locked to the engine shaft. The front cover must rotate with the engine shaft, in the same direction.

Now, since the front cover is bolted to the drum housing, which is locked to the propeller drive sleeve by the disk clutch, there is a complete lock from the engine shaft to the reduction gear shaft. The entire assembly rotates as a unit in the same direction as the engine shaft; this motion gives the propeller a forward rotation.

When the operating lever is thrown into the reverse position, the plungers are withdrawn, and both clutches are disengaged. At the same time, the brake band is tightened around the drum, holding the drum stationary. The bearing cage is locked to the drum. The cone clutch rotates freely out of contact with the front cover. Then the motion from the engine shaft to the reduction gear shaft is transmitted through the inner gear assembly.

The reverse gear pinions are held in the bearing cage, which is stationary for reverse rotation. There are three short pinions, each in mesh with the small inner gear of the engine sleeve. The three short pinions mesh with the three long pinions, each of which also meshes with the propeller drive sleeve gear. Engine rotation is transmitted from the engine sleeve to the short pinions, to the long pinions, and to the propeller drive sleeve. These pinions (gear train) cause the reduction gear shaft to rotate opposite to the engine rotation, and give the propeller a reverse rotation.

The gears are set for reverse rotation, and the brake band is clamped to the drum. The parts, which are shaded, are held stationary by the brake band, and the remaining internal parts, which are not shaded, rotate. (The rotation of the engine shaft and engine sleeve is transmitted directly to the cone clutch and the short pinions. The cone clutch rotates freely out of contact with the stationary front cover. The short pinions drive the long pinions, which drive the propeller drive sleeve. The latter unit is keyed to and drives the reduction gear shaft, which rotates opposite to the engine shaft).

The reduction gear unit is bolted to the reverse gear housing. It consists merely of an external gear, mounted on the reduction gear shaft, and in mesh with a larger internal gear, mounted on the propeller shaft. Power is transferred, at a reduced speed, from the smaller drive gear to the larger internal gear.

Lubrication of the clutch and reverse gear mechanism is accomplished by means of a drilled passage in the crankshaft that supplies oil, as a spray, to the gears and other moving parts. This oil returns to the engine sump by gravity.

An external line from the engine's main oil gallery accomplishes lubrication of the reduction gear unit. Oil is sprayed over the gears and moving parts to lubricate and cool them. Excess oil either drains back to the engine sump by gravity, or, where the unit is below the engine, returns to the sump by means of a scavenging pump.

Airflex Clutch and Gear Assembly

On the larger diesel-propelled ships of the past, the clutch, reverse and reduction gear unit had to transmit an enormous amount of power. To maintain the weight and size of the mechanism as low as possible, special clutches were designed for large diesel installations. One of these was the airflex clutch and gear assembly used with some General Motors engines on Landing Ship, Tanks (LST). These naval vessels were created during World War II to support amphibious operations.

A typical airflex clutch and gear assembly, for ahead and astern rotation could be found with two clutches, one for forward rotation and one for reverse rotation. The clutches were bolted to the engine flywheel by means of a steel spacer, so that they both rotate with the engine at all times, and at engine speed. Each clutch had a flexible tire (or gland) on the inner side of a steel shell. Before the tires were inflated, they rotated out of contact with the drums, which were keyed to the forward and reverse drive shafts. When air under pressure (100 psi) is sent into one of the tires, the inside diameter of the clutch decreases. This causes the friction blocks on the inner tire surface to come in contact with the clutch drum, locking the drive shaft with the engine.

The clutch tire nearest the engine (forward clutch) is inflated to contact and drive the forward drum with the engine. The forward drum is keyed to the forward drive shaft, which carries the double helical forward pinion at the after end of the gear box. The forward pinion is in constant mesh with the double helical main gear, which is keyed on the propeller shaft. By following through the gear train, you can see that, for ahead motion, the propeller rotates in a direction opposite to the engine's rotation.

The reverse clutch is inflated to engage the reverse drum, which is then driven by the engine. The reverse drum is keyed to the short reverse shaft, which surrounds the forward drive shaft. A large reverse step-up pinion transmits the motion to the large reverse step-up gear on the upper shaft. The upper shaft rotation is opposite to the engine's rotation. The main reverse pinion on the upper shaft is in constant mesh with the main gear. By tracing through the gear train, it may be seen that, for reverse rotation, the propeller rotates in the same direction as the engine.

The diameter of the main gear of the airflex clutch is approximately 2 1/2 times as great as that of the forward and reverse pinions. There is a speed reduction of 2 1/2 to 1 from either pinion to the propeller shaft.

Since the forward and main reverse pinions are in constant mesh with the main gear, the set that is not clutched in will rotate as idlers driven from the main gear. The idling gears rotate in a direction opposite to their rotation when carrying the load. For example, with the forward clutch engaged, the main reverse pinion rotates in a direction opposite to its rotation for astern motion. Since the drums rotate in opposite directions, a control mechanism is installed to prevent the engagement of both clutches simultaneously.

An operating lever that works the air control housing, located at the after end of the forward pinion shaft, controls the airflex clutch. The control mechanism directs the high-pressure air into the proper paths to inflate the clutch glands (tires). The air shaft, which connects the control mechanism to the clutches, passes through the forward drive shaft.

The supply air enters the control housing through the air check valve and must pass through the small air orifice. The purpose of the restricted orifice is to delay the inflation of the clutch to be engaged, when shifting from one direction of rotation to the other. The delay is necessary to allow the other clutch to be fully deflated and out of contact with its drum before the inflating clutch can make contact with its drum.

The supply air goes to the rotary air joint in which a hollow carbon cylinder is held to the valve shaft by spring tension. This prevents leakage between the stationary carbon seal and the rotating air valve shaft. The air goes from the rotary joint to the four-way air valve. The sliding-sleeve assembly of the four-way valve can be shifted endwise along the valve shaft by operating the control lever.

When the shifter arm on the control lever slides the valve assembly away from the engine, air is directed to the forward clutch. The four-way valve makes the connection between the air supply and the forward clutch, as follows: there are eight neutral ports which connect the central air supply passage in the valve shaft with the sealed air chamber in the sliding member. In the neutral position of the four-way valve, the air chamber is a dead end for the supply air. In the forward position of the valve, the sliding member uncovers eight forward ports, which connect with the forward passages conducting the air to the forward clutch. The air now flows through the neutral ports, air chamber, forward ports, and forward passages to inflate the forward clutch gland. As long as the valve is in the forward position, the forward clutch will remain inflated and the entire forward air system will remain at a pressure of 100 psi.

Lubrication

On most large gear units, a separate lubrication system is used. Oil is picked up from the gear box by an electric-driven gear-type lubricating oil pump and is sent through a strainer and cooler. After being cleaned and cooled, the oil is returned to the gear box to cool and lubricate the gears. In twin installations, a separate pump is used for each unit and a standby pump is interconnected for emergency use.

Hydraulic Clutches or Couplings

The fluid clutch (coupling) is widely used on Navy ships. The use of hydraulic coupling eliminates the need for a mechanical connection between the engine and the reduction gears. Couplings of this type operate with a minimum of slippage.

Some slippage is necessary for operation of the hydraulic coupling, since torque is transmitted because of the principle of relative motion between the two rotors. The power loss resulting from the small amount of slippage is transformed into heat, which is absorbed by the oil in the system.

Compared with mechanical clutches, hydraulic clutches had a number of advantages. There was no mechanical connection between the driving and driven elements of the hydraulic coupling. Power is transmitted through the coupling very efficiently (97 percent) without transmitting torsional vibrations, or load shocks, from the engine to the reduction gears. This protects the engine, the gears, and the shafting from sudden loads that may occur because of piston seizure or fouling of the propeller. The power is transmitted entirely by the circulation of a driving fluid (oil) between radial passages in a pair of rotors. In addition, the assembly of the hydraulic coupling will absorb or allow for slight misalignment.

The primary rotor (impeller) is attached to the engine crankshaft. The secondary rotor (runner) is attached to the reduction gear pinion shaft. The cover is bolted to the secondary rotor and surrounds the primary rotor. Each rotor is shaped like a half-doughnut with radial partitions. A shallow trough is welded into the partitions around the inner surface of the rotor. The radial passages tunnel under this trough.

When the coupling is assembled, the two rotors are placed facing each other to complete the doughnut. The rotors do not quite touch each other, the clearance between them being 1/4 to 5/8 inch, depending on the size of the coupling. The curved radial passages of the two rotors are opposite each other, so that the outer passages combine to make a circular passage except for the small gaps between the rotors.

In the hydraulic coupling assembly, the driving shaft is secured to the engine crankshaft and the driven shaft goes to the reduction gear box. The oil inlet admits oil directly to the rotor cavities, which become completely filled. The rotor housing is bolted to the secondary rotor and has an oil-sealed joint with the driving shaft. A ring valve, going entirely around the rotor housing, can be operated by the ring valve mechanism to open or close a series of emptying holes housing. When the ring valve is opened, the oil will fly out from the rotor housing into the coupling housing, draining the coupling completely in two or three seconds. Even when the ring valve is closed, some oil leaks out into the coupling housing, and additional oil enters through the inlet. From the coupling housing, the oil is drawn by a pump to a cooler, then sent back to the coupling.

Another coupling assembly used on several Navy ships is the hydraulic coupling with piston-type quick-dumping valves. In this coupling, in which the operation is similar to the one described above, a series of piston valves, around the periphery of the rotor housing, are normally held in the closed position by springs. By means of air oil pressure admitted to the valves, the pistons are moved axially so as to uncover drain ports, allowing the coupling to empty. Where extremely rapid declutching is not required, the piston-valve coupling offers the advantages of greater simplicity and lower cost than the ring-valve coupling.

Another type of self-contained unit for certain diesel engine drives is the scoop control coupling. In couplings of this type, the oil is picked up by one of two scoop tubes (one tube for each direction of rotation), mounted on the external manifold. Each scoop tube contains two passages: a smaller one (outermost) handles the normal flow of oil for cooling and lubrication, and a larger one, which rapidly transfers oil from the reservoir directly to the working circuit.

The scoop tubes are operated from the control stand through a system of linkages. As one tube moves outward from the shaft centerline and into the oil annulus, the other is being retracted.

Four spring-loaded centrifugal valves are mounted on the primary rotor. These valves are arranged to open progressively as the speed of the primary rotor decreases. The arrangement provides the necessary oil flow for cooling as it is required. Quick-emptying piston valves are provided to give rapid emptying of the circuit when the scoop tube is withdrawn from contact with the rotating oil annulus.

Under normal circulating conditions, oil fed into the collector ring passes into the piston valve control tubes. These tubes and connecting passages conduct oil to the outer end of the pistons. The centrifugal force of the oil in the control tube holds the piston against the valve port, thus sealing off the circuit. When the scoop tube is withdrawn from the oil annulus in the reservoir, the circulation of oil will be interrupted and the oil in the control tubes will be discharged through the orifice in the outer end of the piston housing. This releases the pressure on the piston and allows it to move outward, thus opening the port for rapid discharge of oil. Resumption of oil flow from the scoop tube will fill the control tubes; and the pressure will move the piston to the closed position.

When the engine is started and the coupling is filled with oil, the primary rotor turns with the engine crankshaft. As the primary rotor turns, the oil in its radial passages flows outward, under centrifugal force. This forces oil across the gap at the outer edge of the rotor and into the radial passages of the secondary rotor, where the oil flows inward. The oil in the primary rotor is not only flowing outward, but is also rotating. As the oil flows over and into the secondary rotor, it strikes the radial blades in the rotor.

The secondary rotor soon begins to rotate and pick up speed, but it will always rotate more slowly than the primary rotor because of drag on the secondary shaft. Therefore, the centrifugal force of the oil in the primary rotor will always be greater than that of the oil in the secondary rotor. This causes a constant flow from the primary rotor to the secondary rotor at the outer ends of the radial passages, and from the secondary rotor to the primary rotor at the inner ends.

The power loss in the hydraulic clutch is small (3 percent) and is caused by friction in the fluid itself. This means that approximately 97 percent of the power delivered to the primary rotor is transmitted to the reduction gear. The loss power is transformed into heat that is absorbed by the oil—which is the reason for sending part of the oil through a cooler at all times.

Maintenance

Keeping an internal combustion engine (diesel or gasoline) in good operating condition demands a well-planned procedure of periodic inspection, adjustments, maintenance, and repair. If inspections are made regularly, much maladjustment can be detected and corrected before a serious casualty results. A planned maintenance program will help to prevent major casualties and the occurrence of many operating troubles.

There may be times when service requirements interfere with a planned maintenance program. In this event, routine maintenance must be performed as soon as possible after the specified interval of time has elapsed. Necessary corrective measures should be accomplished as soon as possible; if repair jobs are allowed to accumulate, the result may be hurried and incomplete work.

Since the Navy used so many models of internal combustion engines, it was impossible to specify any detailed overhaul procedure that was adaptable to all models. However, there were several general rules that applied to all engines. They were:

1. Detailed repair procedures are listed in manufacturers' instruction manuals and maintenance pamphlets. Study the appropriate manuals and pamphlets before attempting any repair work. Pay particular attention to tolerances, limits, and adjustments.

2. Ensure the highest degree of cleanliness is observed in handling engine parts during overhaul.

3. Before starting repair work, ensure that all required tools and replacements for known defective parts are available.

4. Ensure detailed records of repairs are kept. Such records should include the measurements of parts, hours in use, and new parts installed. An analysis of such records will indicate the hours of operation that may be expected from the various engine parts. This knowledge was helpful as an aid in determining when a part should be renewed in order to avoid a failure.

5. Detailed information on preventive maintenance was contained in the PMS Manual for the engineering department. All preventive maintenance was accomplished in accordance with the (3-M System) Planned Maintenance Subsystem that was based upon the proper utilization of the PMS manuals, Maintenance Requirement Cards (MRCs), and schedules for the accomplishment of planned maintenance actions.

It should be noted that the PMS *does not* cover certain operating checks and inspections that were required as a normal part of the regular watchstanding routine. For example, you will not find such things as hourly pressure and temperature checks or routine oil level checks listed as maintenance requirements under the PMS. Even though these routine operating checks are not listed as PMS requirements, they still had to be performed in accordance with all applicable watchstander's instructions.

CHAPTER 4

GAS TURBINE PLANTS

The gas turbine engine, long regarded as a promising but experimental prime mover, has in recent years been developed to the point where it is entirely practicable for ship propulsion and for a number of auxiliary applications. Gas turbine engines were installed as prime movers on minesweepers, landing craft, PT boats, air-sea rescue boats, hydrofoils, hydroskimmers, and other craft. In addition, the gas turbine engine found increasing application as the driving unit for ship's service generators, pumps, and other auxiliary units.

Although the gas turbine engine as a type need no longer be regarded as experimental, many specific models of gas turbine engines were still at least partially experimental and subject to further change and development. The discussion in this chapter therefore deals primarily with the general principles of gas turbine engines (before the Aegis Cruisers) rather than with specific models. Detailed information on any specific model may be obtained from the manufacturer's technical manual furnished with the equipment.

Basic Principles

The gas turbine engine bears some resemblance to an internal combustion engine of the reciprocating type and some resemblance to a steam turbine. However, a brief consideration of the basic principles of a gas turbine engine reveals several ways in which the gas turbine engine is quite unlike either the reciprocating internal combustion engine or the steam turbine.

Let us look first at the thermodynamic cycles of the three engine types. The reciprocating internal combustion engine has an open, heated-engine cycle and the steam turbine has a closed, unheated-engine cycle. In contrast, the gas turbine has an open, unheated-engine cycle—a combination we have not previously encountered in our study of naval machinery. The gas turbine cycle is *open* because it includes the atmosphere; it is an *unheated-engine cycle* because the working substance is heated in a device, which is separate from the engine.

Another way in which the three types of engines differ is in the working substance. The working fluid in a steam turbine installation is steam. In both the reciprocating internal combustion engine and the gas turbine engine, the working fluid may be considered as being the hot gases of combustion that result from the burning of fuel in air. However, there are very important differences in the way the working fluid is used in the reciprocating internal combustion engine and in the gas turbine engine.

Still other differences in the three types of engines become apparent when we consider the arrangement and relationship of component parts and the processes that occur during the cycle. From our study of previous chapters of this text, we are already familiar with the functional arrangement of parts in steam turbine installations and in reciprocating internal combustion engines. Now let us discuss the relationship of the major components in a basic gas turbine engine.

In the steam turbine installation, the processes of combustion and steam generation take place in the boiler, while the process by which the thermal energy of the steam is converted into mechanical work takes place in the turbine. In the reciprocating internal combustion engine, three processes—the compression of atmospheric air, the combustion of a fuel-air mixture, and the conversion of heat to work—all take place in one unit, the cylinder. The gas turbine engine is similar to the reciprocating internal combustion engine in that the same three processes—compression, combustion, and conversion of heat to work—occur; but it is unlike the reciprocating internal combustion engine in that these three processes take place in three separate units rather than in one unit. In the gas turbine engine, the compression of atmospheric air is accomplished in the compressor; the combustion of fuel is accomplished in the combustion chamber; and the conversion of heat to work is accomplished in the turbine.

Many different types and models of earlier gas turbine engines were in use: a *single-shaft* type because one shaft from the turbine rotor drives the compressor and an extension of this same shaft drives the load; and a *split-shaft type*. The split-shaft type was considered to be split into two sections: the gas-producing section, or gas generator, and the power turbine section. The gas-generator section, in which a stream of expanding gases is created as a result of continuous combustion, includes the compressor, the combustion chamber (or chambers), and the gas-generator turbine. The power turbine section consists of a power turbine and the power output shaft. In this type of gas turbine engine, there is no mechanical connection between the gas-generator turbine and the power turbine. When the engine is operating, the two turbines produce the same effect as that produced by a hydraulic torque converter. The split-shaft gas turbine engine is well suited for use as a propulsion unit where loads vary, since the gas-generator section can be operated at a steady and continuous speed while the power turbine section is free to vary with the load. Starting effort required for a split-shaft gas turbine engine is far less than that required for a single-shaft gas turbine engine connected to the reduction gear, propulsion shaft, and propeller.

In the twin-spool gas turbine engine the air compressor is split into two sections or stages and each stage is driven by a separate turbine element. The low-pressure turbine element drives the low-pressure compressor element and the high-pressure turbine element drives the high-pressure compressor element. Like the split-shaft type, the twin-spool gas turbine engine is usually divided into a gas-generator section and a power turbine section. However, some twin-spool gas turbine engines are so arranged that the low-pressure turbine element drives the low-pressure compressor element and the power output shaft.

The basic cycle of the gas turbine engine is one of isentropic compression, constant-pressure heat addition, isentropic expansion, and constant-pressure heat rejection. As the hot combustion gases are expanded through the turbine, converting thermal energy into mechanical work, some of the turbine work is used to drive the compressor and the remainder is used to drive the load. The power output from the turbine is steady and continuous and, after the initial start, self-sustaining.

Although this chapter deals only with earlier gas turbine engines, which operated on the simple open cycle, it should be mentioned that other cycles are also of interest to designers of gas turbine engines. Among the cycles that have been considered (and to some extent used) are the closed cycle, the semi-open cycle, and various modifications of the simple open cycle. In one such modification, known as the *regenerated open cycle*, the hot exhaust gases from the turbine are passed through a heat exchanger in which they give up some heat to the air between the compressor discharge and the inlet to the combustion chamber. The utilization of this heat decreases the amount of fuel required and there-by increases the efficiency of the cycle.

FUNCTIONS OF COMPONENTS

As we have seen, the three major components of a gas turbine engine are the compressor, the combustion chamber, and the turbine. In addition, the engine requires a number of other components, accessories, and systems in order to operate as a complete unit. The functions of the gas turbine engine components are described in the following sections.

Compressor

The compressor takes in atmospheric air and compresses it to a pressure of several atmospheres. Part of the compressed air, called primary air, enters directly into the combustion chamber where it is mixed with the atomized fuel so that the mixture can be ignited and burned. The remainder of the air, called secondary air, is mixed with the gases of combustion. The purpose of the secondary air is to cool the combustion gases down to the desired turbine inlet temperature.

Both axial-flow compressors and centrifugal (radial-flow) compressors are currently used in gas turbine engines. There are several possible configurations of these basic types, some of which are in use and some of which are in experimental phases of development.

In the axial-flow compressor, the air is compressed as it flows axially along the shaft. An axial-flow compressor of good design may achieve efficiencies in the range of 82 to 88 percent at compressor pressure ratios up to 8:1. At higher pressure ratios, the efficiency tends to decrease. Axial flow compressors may be of the single-spool type. The gas turbine engine has an axial-flow compressor of the single-spool type. The axial-flow single-spool compressor can be removed from its engine. Where twin-spool axial-flow compressors are used, a separate turbine drives each spool.

The centrifugal (radial-flow) compressor picks up the entering air and accelerates it outward by means of centrifugal force. The centrifugal compressor may achieve efficiencies of 80 to 84 percent at pressure ratios of 2.5 to 4 and efficiencies of 76 to 81 percent at pressure ratios of 4 to 10.

The advantages of the axial-flow compressor include high peak efficiencies; a relatively small frontal area for any given air flow; and only negligible losses between stages, even when a large number of stages are used. The disadvantages of the axial-flow compressor include difficulty of manufacture, high initial cost, and relatively great weight.

The advantages of the centrifugal compressor include a high-pressure rise per stage, simplicity of manufacture, low initial cost, and relatively lightweight. The disadvantages of the centrifugal compressor include the need for a relatively large frontal area for a given air flow and the difficulty of using two or more stages because of losses that would occur between the stages.

Combustion Chamber

The combustion chamber is the component in which the fuel-air mixture is burned. The combustion chamber consists of a casing, a perforated inner shell, a fuel nozzle, and a device for initial ignition. The number of combustion chambers used in a gas turbine engine varies widely; as few as one and as many as sixteen combustion chambers have been used in one gas turbine engine.

The combustion chamber is the most efficient component of a gas turbine engine. Efficiencies between 95 and 98 percent can be obtained over a wide operating range. To produce such efficiencies, combustion chambers are designed to operate with low-pressure losses, high combustion efficiency, and good flame stability. Additional requirements for the combustion chamber include low rates of carbon formation, lightweight, reliability, reasonable length of life, and the ability to mix cold air with the hot combustion gases in such a way as to give uniform temperature distribution to the turbine blades.

Only a small part (perhaps one-fourth) of the air that enters the combustion chamber area is burned with the fuel. The remainder of the air is used to keep the temperature of the combustion gases low enough so that the turbine nozzles and blades will not be overheated and thereby damaged.

The basic types of combustion chambers in current use are the tubular or can-type chamber, the annular chamber, the can-annular chamber, and the elbow chamber.

The tubular or can-type chamber, is used with both axial-flow and centrifugal compressors. The can-type combustion chamber consists of an outer case or housing within which is a perforated, stainless steel, highly heat resistant combustion chamber liner. The combustion chamber housing is divided to facilitate liner replacement. Each can-type chamber has its own individual air inlet duct.

Interconnector tubes (flame tubes) are a necessary part of can-type combustion chambers.

Since each of the combustion chambers has its own separate burner, each one operating independently of the others, there must be some way to spread the flames during starting. This requirement is met by interconnecting all the chambers so that, as the spark ignition plugs in the lower chambers start the flame, the flame passes through the interconnector tubes and ignites the combustible mixture in the adjacent chambers. Once ignition is obtained, the spark igniters are automatically cut off.

The annular combustion chamber is more efficient than the can-type chamber. Although details of design may vary, the annular combustion chamber consists essentially of a single chamber that completely surrounds the engine. Fuel enters the combustion chamber through a series of nozzles which are mounted equidistant from each other on a ring at the front end of the combustion chamber; because of this arrangement, the flame is distributed evenly around the entire circumference of the combustion chamber. Diffusion of air and an efficient flame pattern are maintained by means of rows of holes that are punched in the outer liner or basket of the combustion chamber.

The can-annular combustion chamber combines features of both the can-type chamber and the annular chamber. The can-annular chamber allows an annular discharge from the compressors, from which the air flows to individual burners where the fuel is injected and burned. The can-annular combustion chambers are arranged radially around the axis of the engine—the axis in this instance being the rotor shaft housing.

The can-annular combustion chambers are enclosed by a removable steel shroud, which covers the entire burner section. This feature makes the burners readily accessible for any required maintenance.

The can-annular combustion chambers are interconnected by means of projecting flame tubes. These flame tubes facilitate starting, as previously described in connection with the can-type combustion chamber.

Each of the can-annular combustion chambers contains a central, bullet-shaped, perforated liner. The size and shape of the holes are designed to admit the correct quantity of air at the required velocity and angle. Cutouts are provided in two of the bottom chambers for the installation of the spark igniters.

Each can-annular combustion chamber receives fuel through duplex nozzles installed at the forward end of the chamber. Guide vanes around the fuel nozzles direct the primary air and cause it to enter the combustion chamber with a swirling motion, which mixes the fuel and air and thus leads to even and complete combustion.

Turbine

In theory, design, and operating characteristics, the turbines used in gas turbine engines are quite similar to the turbines used in a steam plant. The gas turbine differs from the steam turbine chiefly in the type of blading material used, the means provided for cooling the bearings and highly stressed parts, and the higher ratio of blade length to wheel diameter, which is required to accommodate the large gas flow.

The turbine section of a gas turbine engine is located directly behind the combustion chamber outlet. The turbine consists of two basic elements, the *stator* and the *rotor*.

The stator element is referred to by various names, including *turbine nozzle vanes* and *turbine guide vanes*. The vanes of the stator element serve the same purpose as the nozzles in an impulse steam turbine or the stationary blading in a reaction steam turbine—that is, they convert thermal energy into mechanical kinetic energy. The vanes of the stator element are contoured and set at such an angle that they form a number of small nozzles that discharge the gas as extremely high-speed jets. As in the case of the nozzles (or stationary blading) of steam turbines, the increase in velocity may be equated with the decrease in thermal energy. The vanes of the stator element direct the flow of gas to the rotor blades at the required angle while the turbine wheel is rotating.

The rotor element of the turbine consists of a shaft and a bladed wheel or disk. The wheel is attached to the main power transmitting shaft of the gas turbine engine. The jets of combustion gas leaving the vanes of the stator element act upon the turbine blades and cause the turbine wheel to rotate at a very high rate of speed. The high rotational speed imposes severe centrifugal loads on the turbine wheel, and at the same time, the very high temperatures result in a lowering of the strength of the material. Consequently, the engine speed and temperature must be controlled to keep turbine operation within safe limits. Even so, the operating life of the turbine blading is accepted as the governing factor in determining the life of the gas turbine engine.

The turbine may be of the single-rotor type or of the multiple-rotor type. Either single-rotor or multiple-rotor turbines may be used with either centrifugal or axial-flow compressors. In the single-rotor type of turbine, the power is developed by one rotor and this single wheel drives all engine-driven parts. In the multiple-rotor type, two or more rotors develop the power. It is possible for one or more rotors to drive the compressor and the accessories, while one or more other rotors are used for the power output.

Main Bearings

The main bearings in a gas turbine engine serve the critical function of supporting the compressor, the turbine, and the engine shaft. The number and position of main bearings required for proper support vary according to the length and stiffness of the shaft, with both length and stiffness being affected by the type of compressor used in the engine. In general, a gas turbine engine requires at least three main bearings and may require six or even more.

Several types of main bearings are used in gas turbine engines. Ball and roller bearings have been quite commonly used in the past, and they are still used in many aircraft gas turbine engines. Sleeve bearings, split-sleeve bearings, floating-sleeve bearings, and slipper bearings are commonly used in gas turbine engines designed for marine propulsion.

The slipper or pivoted-shoe type of bearing has recently attracted considerable attention and is being used increasingly for main bearings on gas turbine engines and other high speed engines. This type of bearing is designed with relatively large radial clearances. Since a rotating object tends to rotate about its true balance center when it is not restrained by bearings or supports, the large radial clearances in the slipper bearings allow a kind of self-balancing action or automatic compensation for balance errors to take place when the engine is operating.

In one type of slipper bearing, the slipper consists of four pivoted-shoe segments, similar to the pivoted shoes used in Kingsbury bearings. The segments are held together loosely by a wire spring.

In another type of slipper bearing, the slipper consists of six segments, which are fastened in place by dowel pins. This type of bearing is sometimes called a fixed-pivot slipper bearing.

Accessory Drives

Because the turbine and the compressor are on the same rotating shaft, a popular misconception is that the gas turbine engine has only one moving part. This is not the case, however. A gas turbine engine requires a starting device (which is usually a moving part), some kind of control mechanism, and power take-offs.

The accessory drive section of the gas turbine engine takes care of these various accessory functions. The primary purpose of the accessory drive section is to provide space for the mounting of the accessories required for the operation and control of the engine. Secondary purposes include acting as an oil reservoir and/or oil sump and providing for and housing accessory drive gears and reduction gears.

The engine rotor through an accessory drive shaft gear coupling drives the gear train.

The reduction gearing within the case provides suitable drive speeds for each engine accessory or component. Because the operating rpm of the rotor is so high, the accessory reduction gear ratios are relatively high. Ball bearings assembled in the mounting bores of the accessory case support the accessory drives.

Accessories always provided in the accessory drive section include the fuel control, with its governing device; the high-pressure fuel oil pump or pumps; the oil sump; the oil pressure and scavenging pump or pumps; the auxiliary fuel pump; and a starter. Additional accessories which may be included in the accessory drive section or which may be provided elsewhere include a starting fuel pump, a hydraulic oil pump, a generator, and a tachometer. Some gas turbine engines are equipped with magnetos for ignition and these magnetos are driven from the accessory drive. Most of these accessories are essential for the operation and control of any gas turbine engine; however, the particular combination and arrangement of engine-driven accessories depends upon the use for which the gas turbine engine is designed.

Engine Systems

The major systems of a gas turbine engine are those that supply fuel, lubricating oil, and electricity.

Fuel System

The fuel system supplies the specified fuel for combustion. The components of a fuel system depend to some extent upon the type of gas turbine engine; however, the basic fuel oil system may be regarded as typical of a simple fuel system. The engine-driven pump receives filtered fuel from a motor-driven supply pump at a constant pressure. The engine-driven fuel pump increases the pressure and forces the fuel through the high-pressure filter to the fuel control governor in the fuel control assembly. The fuel control governor provides fuel to the nozzles at the pressure and volume required to maintain the desired engine performance. At the same time, the fuel control governor limits fuel flow to maintain operating conditions within safe limits.

The fuel nozzles serve to introduce the fuel into the combustion chamber. The fuel is sprayed into the combustion chamber under pressure, through small orifices in the nozzles. Various kinds of fuel nozzles are in use. The simplex nozzle was used on some older gas turbine engines. Most recent gas turbine engines use some kind of duplex nozzle. A duplex nozzle requires a dual manifold just ahead of the nozzles and a flow divider (before the manifold) to divide the fuel into primary and secondary streams. The duplex type of nozzle provides a desirable spray pattern for combustion over twice the range of that provided by the simplex nozzle.

The fuel control assembly is the unit, which regulates the turbine rpm by adjusting fuel flow from the high-pressure engine-driven pump to the fuel nozzle. Fuel enters the fuel control assembly and is pumped through a filter. High-pressure fuel is routed to the differential relief valve, then to the fuel shutoff valve, and finally to the fuel nozzles.

The speed-setting lever on the outboard end of the governor is connected to a speed control device on the control console either by a cable or by an electric servomotor. At the fuel control end, the lever is keyed to a pinion. This pinion positions a rack, which in turn controls the governor flyweight spring. The mechanism regulates gas producer speed according to the position of the control lever. With the control lever in any particular position, the governor flyweights sense variations from the preset speed and a compensating movement of the fuel control valve results. An externally adjustable needle valve provides a constant minimum fuel flow during deceleration, when the governor valve is closed, to prevent loss of combustion. An acceleration limiter, consisting of a needle valve positioned by a shaft, arm, and bellows, is actuated by compressor discharge pressure. During acceleration, this mechanism controls fuel flow to the point at which the governor flyweight mechanism and its fuel control valve take over.

Lubricating System

Because of the high operating rpm and the high operating temperatures encountered in gas turbine engines, proper lubrication is of vital importance. The lubricating system is designed to supply bearings and gears with clean lubricating oil at the desired pressures and temperatures. In some installations, the lubricating system also furnishes oil to various hydraulic systems. Heat absorbed by the lubricating oil is transferred to the cooling medium in a lube oil cooler.

The lubricating system has a combined hydraulic system—in this case; the hydraulic system is for the operation of a hydraulic clutch in a gas turbine propulsion system. The lubricating system illustrated is of the dry-sump type, with a common oil supply from an externally mounted oil tank. The system includes the oil tank, the lubricating oil pump, the hydraulic oil pump, the air inlet scavenging pump, the oil temperature switch, the oil cooler, oil filters, the pressure regulating valve, the diverter valve, and a low-pressure switch.

All bearings and gears in the engine, accessory drives, reduction gears, and reverse gear are lubricated and cooled by the lubricating system. In addition, the system supplies oil for the lubrication of the fuel control governor.

Electrical System

In the gas turbine engine, the electrical system is the principal means of automatic control of the engine. Electrical circuits, which incorporate speed and pressure sensing switches, control the starting and ignition sequence by opening and closing various valves in the fuel system. Engine operating conditions are reported by speed, pressure, and temperature operated switches and temperature bulbs.

The electrical system usually includes a starter, an ignition circuit, a control battery, and relays. In addition, it includes electrical accessories and control components such as the starting and ignition control switches and relays; the panel-mounted instruments and indicator lights for oil temperature, oil pressure, and engine rpm; and engine-mounted reporting devices such as fuel pressure switches, oil temperature switches, oil pressure switches, and thermo-couples.

The starting and ignition circuits receive power from storage batteries. The warning and safety circuits receive power from the ship's power supply panel. Power for the indicating circuits is self-generated by thermocouples and other units in the circuits.

Engine Starters

Of the various methods used for starting gas turbine engines, the three most common devices are the air turbine, the hydraulic starting device, and the electric starter-generator.

The air turbine starter is a turbine-air motor with a radial inward-flow turbine wheel assembly and an engaging and disengaging mechanism. Compressed air is supplied to the air turbine from an external source.

The hydraulic motor starter consists of a motor-driven hydraulic pump mounted separately. It supplies high-pressure hydraulic oil to the hydraulic motor starter, which is mounted on the accessory pad along with its engaging and disengaging mechanism. The hydraulic motor starter is quite similar to the air turbine starter; however, the hydraulic motor starter is usually used for larger and higher horsepower gas turbine engines.

The electric starter-generator is a shunt-wound DC generator with compensating windings and a series winding, using a 24-volt battery power source. The generator is usually mounted on the accessory drive pad. The generator is so designed and controlled that it can be used as an engine starter. When the designed engine speed is reached, the starter-generator is automatically switched from a starter to a generator.

Transmission of Engine Power

The two main types of gas turbine engine installations used for ship propulsion are (1) the geared drive, and (2) the turboelectric drive.

The fundamental characteristics of the earlier gas turbine engine make it necessary for the drive mechanism to change both the speed and the direction of shaft rotation in the driven mechanism. The process of transmitting engine power to a point where it can be used in performing useful work involves a number of factors, two of which are torque and speed. The gas turbine engine does not produce high torque, but it does produce high speed. Therefore, a gear train is used with most gas turbine engines to lower speed and increase torque. This is true in both types of installations. In the case of the geared drive installation, the gears are used between the gas turbine engine and the propeller shaft. In the case of the turboelectric drive, the gears are usually used between the gas turbine engine and the generator shaft, to reduce the rpm of the generator to a practicable operating value.

The propelling equipment of a boat or ship must be capable of providing reversing power as well as forward power. In a few ships and boats, reversing is accomplished by the use of controllable pitch propellers. In most vessels, however, reversing is accomplished by the use of reversing gears.

Reducing the speed of rotation and reversing the direction of shaft rotation are not the only requirements of the drive mechanism of a ship or boat. It is also necessary to make some provision for the fact that the engine must be able to operate at times without transmitting power to the propeller shaft. In the electric drive, this is no problem because the transmission of power is controlled electrically. With the gear type of drive, however, it is necessary to include a means of disconnecting the engine from the propeller shaft. Devices used for this purpose are called *clutches.*

The arrangement of components in a gear-type drive varies, depending upon the type and size of the installation. In some of the small installations, the clutch, the reversing gear, and the reduction gear may be combined in a single unit. In other installations, the clutch and the reversing gear may be in one housing and the reduction gear in a separate housing attached to the reversing gear housing. Drive mechanisms arranged in either manner are called *transmissions.*

Gas Turbine Engines and Jet Propulsion

Thus far, we have considered the gas turbine engine as a prime mover, which delivers power in the form of torque on an output shaft. In concluding this chapter, it should be noted that the gas turbine engine also serves as the prime mover in the power plants of many military aircraft. When so adapted, the gas turbine engine develops power by converting thermal energy into mechanical kinetic energy in a high velocity gas stream. The highly accelerated gas stream creates *thrust*, which propels the aircraft. This method of creating thrust is called the *direct reaction* or *jet propulsion method*.

The concept of thrust is basic to an understanding of jet propulsion. The concept of thrust is based on Newton's third law of motion, which may be stated as follows: *For every acting force there is an equal and opposite reacting force*. In the case of aircraft in flight, the acting force is the force the engine exerts on the air mass as it flows through the engine. The reacting force (thrust) is the force, which the air mass exerts on the components of the engine as the heated air mass is discharged from the jet nozzle at the rear of the airplane. In other words, thrust is not produced by the ejected air mass reacting against the atmosphere; rather, thrust is created within the engine as the air mass flowing through the engine is accelerated and discharged.

Engines which include the gas turbine and which create thrust by the direct reaction method are commonly identified as turbojet engines. Except for a diffuser and a different type exhaust system in engines of the turbojet type, the basic components of the turbojet engine are similar in design and function to the components of any open-cycle gas turbine engine. The function of the diffuser is to decrease the velocity of the inlet air and to increase its pressure before the air enters the compressor. The exhaust system of a turbojet engine consists of a cone and a convergent nozzle. The exhaust cone is designed to exhaust to the nozzle the accelerated air mass, which the other components of the engine deliver to the cone. As the accelerated air mass flows through the convergent nozzle, its velocity is greatly increased and thrust is created within the engine.

Maintenance

The maintenance of the earlier gas turbines was the normal function of operating activities. Cleanliness was one of the most important basic essentials in operation and maintenance of these gas turbines. Particular care was exercised in keeping fuel, air, coolants, lubricants, rotating elements, and combustion chambers clean. Periodic inspection procedures were followed in order to detect maladjustments, possible failures, and excessive clearances of moving parts. All inspection and maintenance requirements were accomplished in accordance with the 3-M System (PMS Subsystem).

Caution: Never use lead pencils for marking gas turbine hot parts, because the carbon content of the pencil lead caused the stainless steel to become brittle, causing a possible failure of the parts that were marked. A grease pencil was used in marking gas turbine parts. Steel wool was not used to clean gas turbine parts, unless the wool was stainless steel.

The Naval Ship Systems Command set up overhaul periods and procedures. These periods and procedures were reported to the Fleet through Naval Ship's Technical Manuals and/or direct correspondence. Accurate operating logs were kept on each engine so the number of hours and operational history on each engine was readily known. These records aided in developing measures that improved engine reliability.

CHAPTER 5

NUCLEAR POWER PLANTS

N uclear reactors release nuclear energy by the fission process
and transform this energy into thermal energy. While we are
learning more daily about the phenomena, which occur in nuclear
reactions, the knowledge already gained has been put to use in both the
submarine and the surface fleets. In 1955, the first Navy vessel to use
nuclear fission for propulsion was the attack submarine *USS Nautilus*
(SSN 571). Since then, the nuclear engineering field has been in the
stage of rapid development. Today, the use of nuclear propulsion has
greatly expanded to include attack and ballistic missile submarines,
guided missile cruisers and aircraft carriers. However, the discussion
in this chapter is limited to the basic concepts to reactor principles.
The discussion of nuclear physics is limited to the fission process,
since all power reactors in operation during 1955 through 1990 used
the fissioning of a heavy element to release nuclear energy.

Advantages of Nuclear Power

A major advantage of nuclear power for any naval ship is that less
logistic support is required. On ships using conventional petroleum
fuels as an energy source, the cruising range and strategic value are
limited by the amount of fuel that can be stored in their hulls. A ship
of this type must either return to port to take on fuel or refuel at
sea—an operation which is time consuming and hazardous.

Nuclear-powered ships have virtually unlimited cruising range,
since the refueling is done routinely as part of a regular scheduled
overhaul. On her first nuclear fuel load, the *USS Nautilus* steamed
62,562 miles, more than half of this distance fully submerged. The
USS Enterprise steamed over 200,000 miles before being refueled.

In 1963, Operation Sea Orbit, a 30,000-mile cruise around the world in 65 days, completely without logistic support of any kind. It proved conclusively the strategic and tactical flexibility of a nuclear-powered task force.

There are other (and perhaps less obvious) advantages of nuclear power for aircraft carriers. For one thing, tanks that would otherwise be used to store boiler fuels can be used on nuclear-powered carriers to store additional aircraft fuels, giving the ship a greater striking potential. Another advantage is the lack of stacks; since there are no stack gases to cause turbulence in the flight deck atmosphere, the operation of aircraft is less hazardous than on conventionally powered ships.

The fact that a nuclear-powered ship requires no outside source of oxygen from the earth's atmosphere means that the ship can be completely closed off, thereby reducing the hazards of any nuclear attack. This greatly increases the potential of the submarine fleet by giving it the capability of staying submerged for extended periods. In 1960, the nuclear-powered submarine *USS Triton* completed a submerged circumnavigation of the world, traveling a distance of 35,979 miles in 83 days and 10 hours.

Nuclear Fundamentals

At the present time there are 103 known elements of which the smallest particle that can be separated by chemical means is the *atom*. The Rutherford-Bohr theory of atomic structure describes the atom as being similar to our solar system. At the center of every atom is a nucleus which is comparable with the sun; moving in orbits around the nucleus are a number of particles called electrons. The electrons have a negative charge and are held in orbit by the attraction of the positively charged nucleus.

Two elementary particles, *protons* and *neutrons*, often referred to as *nucleons*, compose the atomic nucleus. The positive charge of atomic nuclei is attributed to the protons. A proton has an electrical charge equal and opposite to that of an electron. A neutron has no charge.

The number of electrons in an atom and their relative orbital positions predict how an element will react chemically, whereas the number of protons in an atom determines which element it is. An atom, which is not ionized, contains an equal number of protons and electrons; it is said to be neutral, since the total atomic charge is zero.

The hydrogen atom has a single proton in the nucleus and a single orbital electron. Hydrogen, the lightest element, is said to have a mass of approximately one. The next heavier atom, that of helium, had a mass of four relative to hydrogen and was expected to contain four protons. It was found that the helium atom has only two protons instead of the four expected; the remainder of its mass is attributed to two neutrons located in the nucleus of the helium atom. The more complex atoms contain more protons and neutrons in the nucleus, with a corresponding increase in the number of planetary electrons. The planetary electrons are arranged in orbits or shells of definite energy levels outside the nucleus.

The characteristics of the elementary atomic particles can be compiled and the mass of a proton is much greater than that of an electron; it takes about 1,847 electrons to weigh as much as one hydrogen proton.

It is possible for atoms of the same element to have different numbers of neutrons, and therefore different masses. Atoms, which have the same atomic number (number of protons in the atom), but different masses are called *isotopes*. The atomic mass number identifies different isotopes of the same element, which is the total number of neutrons and protons contained within the nucleus of the atom.

The element hydrogen has three known isotopes. The simplest and most common known form of hydrogen consists of 1 proton, which is the nucleus, and 1 orbital electron. Another form of hydrogen, deuterium, consists of 1 proton and 1 neutron forming the nucleus. The third form, tritium, consists of 1 proton and 2 neutrons forming the nucleus and 1 orbital electron.

In scientific notation, the three isotopes of hydrogen are written as follows:

$$\text{Common hydrogen} \ldots\ldots\ldots\ldots\ldots\ldots {}^{1}_{1}\text{H}$$

$$\text{Deuterium} \ldots\ldots\ldots\ldots\ldots\ldots\ldots {}^{2}_{1}\text{H}$$

$$\text{Tritium} \ldots\ldots\ldots\ldots\ldots\ldots\ldots {}^{3}_{1}\text{H}$$

In this notation, the subscript preceding the symbol of the element indicates the atomic number of the element. The superscript following the symbol of the element is the atomic mass number; thus, the superscript indicates which isotope of the element is being referred to.

The general symbol for any atom is

$$^{A}_{Z}X$$

where

$X =$	symbol of the element
$Z =$	atomic number (number of protons)
$A =$	atomic mass number (sum of the number of protons and the number of neutrons)

Of the known 103 elements, there are approximately 1,000 isotopes, most of which are radioactive.

Radioactivity

All isotopes with atomic number Z greater than 83 are naturally radioactive and many more isotopes can be made artificially radioactive by bombarding with neutrons, which upset the neutron-proton ratio of the normally stable nucleus.

Naturally, radioactive isotopes undergo radioactive decomposition, thereby forming lighter and more stable nuclei. Radioactive decomposition occurs through the emission of an alpha particle or a beta particle. One or more gamma rays may also be emitted with the alpha or beta particle.

An alpha particle (symbol a) is composed of two protons and two neutrons. It is the nucleus of a helium ($^4_2$He) atom, has an electrical charge of +2, and is very stable. In the decay process to a more stable element, many unstable nuclei emit an alpha particle. The results of alpha emission can be seen from the following equation:

$$^{238}_{92}U \longrightarrow \; ^4_2\alpha + \; ^{234}_{90}Th$$

In the above equation, the parent isotope of uranium ($^{238}_{92}U$) is a naturally occurring, radioactive isotope, which decays by alpha emission. Since the A and Z numbers must balance in a nuclear reaction equation, and since an alpha particle contains two protons, we see that the uranium has changed to an entirely new element.

The radioactive isotope of thorium ($^{234}_{90}$Th) produced in the above reaction further (decays by the emission of a negative beta particle symbol -β) as indicated in the following equation:

$$^{234}_{90}Th \longrightarrow \; ^{\;\;0}_{-1}\beta + \; ^{234}_{91}Pa$$

The negative beta particle has properties comparable to an electron. However, the origin of the beta particle is within the nucleus rather than the orbital shells of an atom. It is postulated that a negative beta particle is emitted at an extremely high energy level when a neutron within the nucleus decays to a proton and an electron (the negative beta particle). When this phenomenon occurs, the proton stays within the nucleus forming an isotope of a different element having the same mass. This negative beta decay occurs in nuclei that have fewer protons than stable nuclei having the same total number of neutrons and protons.

A radioactive isotope may go through several transformations of the above types before reaching a stable state. In the case of ($^{238}_{92}U$) there are a total of eight alpha particles and six beta particles emitted prior to reaching a stable isotope of lead ($^{206}_{82}$Pb).

The third manner in which a naturally radioactive isotope may reach a more stable configuration is by the emission of gamma rays (symbol τ). The gamma ray is an electromagnetic type of radiation having frequency, high energy, and a short wave length. Gamma rays are similar to X rays in that the properties are the same. The distinguishing factor between the two is the fact that gamma rays are originated in the nucleus of an atom, whereas the X ray originates from the orbital electrons. In general, it can be said that a gamma ray is of higher energy, higher frequency, and shorter wavelength than an X ray.

Frequently, an isotope which emits an alpha or beta particle in the decay process will emit one or more gamma rays at the same time, as in the cobalt $(_{27}^{60}Co)$ an isotope that decays by beta emission and at the same time emits two gamma rays of different energy levels. Some radioactive isotopes reach a stable state by the emission of gamma rays only. In the latter case, since gamma rays have neither mass nor electrical charge, the A and Z numbers of the isotope remain unchanged but the energy level of the nucleus is reduced.

An important property of any radioactive isotope is the time involved in radioactive decay. To understand the time element, it is necessary to understand the concept of *half-life*. Half-life may be defined as the time required for one-half of any given number of radioactive atoms to disintegrate, thus reducing the radiation intensity of that particular isotope by one-half. Half-lives may vary from microseconds to billions of years. At times, an isotope may be said to be "short-lived" or "long-lived," depending upon its peculiar radioactive half-life. Some half-lives of typical elements are:

$$_{92}U^{238} = 4.51 \times 10^9 \text{ years}$$

$$_{92}U^{235} = 7.13 \times 10^8 \text{ years}$$

$$_{88}Ra^{226} = 1620 \text{ years}$$

$$_{53}I^{135} = 6.7 \text{ hours}$$

$$_{84}Po^{214} = 10^{-6} \text{ seconds}$$

As stated previously, naturally radioactive isotopes decay by the emission of alpha particles, beta particles, gamma rays, or a combination thereof. In the case of induced nuclear reactions, there are many other phenomena, which may occur, including fission and the emission of neutrons, protons, neutrons, and other forms of energy.

Conservation of Mass and Energy

It now becomes necessary to consider mass and energy as two phases of the same principle. In so doing, the law of conservation becomes:

(mass + energy) before = (mass + energy) after.

Fundamental to the above and to the entire subject of nuclear power is Einstein's mass-energy equation where the following relation holds:

$$E = mc^2$$

where

$E =$	energy in ergs,
$m =$	mass in grams,
$c =$	velocity of light (3×10^{10} cm/sec).

Mass and energy are not conserved separately but can be converted into each other.

Several units and conversion factors, which have become conventional to the field of nuclear engineering, are listed below.

1 eV (electronvolt)	= the energy acquired by an electron as it moves through a potential difference of 1 volt
1 MeV (million electron-volt)	= 106eV = 1.52×10^{-16}Btu
1 amu (atomic mass unit)	= 1/12 the mass of a $^{12}_{6}C$ atom (by definition)
1 amu	= 1.49×10^{-3}erg = 1.66×10^{-24}g = 931 MeV = 1.41×10^{-13} Btu

Nuclear Energy Source

It was previously stated that the atomic mass number is the total number of nucleons within the nucleus. It can also be said that the atomic mass number is the nearest integer (as found by experiment) to the actual mass of an isotope. In nuclear equations, the entire mass must be accounted for; therefore, the actual mass must be considered.

The atomic mass of any isotope is somewhat less than indicated by the sum of the individual masses of the protons, neutrons, and orbital electrons, which are the components of that isotope. This difference is termed *mass defect*: it is equivalent to the *binding energy* of the nucleus. Binding energy may be defined as the amount of energy, which was released when a nucleus was formed from its component parts.

The binding energy of any isotope may be found, as in the following example of copper ($_{29}^{63}$Cu) which contains 34 neutrons, 29 protons, and 29 electrons. Using the values given in the characteristics of elementary particles:

Particle	Charge	Mass (amu)
Proton	+1	1.00758
Neutron	0	1.00894
Electron	-1	0.00055

we find:

34 x 1.00894 = 34.30496 amu
29 x 1.00758 = 29.21982 amu
29 x 0.00055 = 0.01595 amu

Total of component masses = 63.54073 amu
    Less actual mass of atom = 62.9298 amu
    Mass defect = 0.61093 amu

Converting to energy, we find:
931 MeV/amu x 0.61093 amu = 568.77583 MeV, or 560.8 ÷ 63 = 8.9 MeV/nucleon

Since binding energy was released when a nucleus was formed from its component parts, it is necessary to add energy to separate a nucleus. In the fissioning of uranium-235, the additional energy is supplied by bombarding the fissionable fuel with neutrons. The fissionable material absorbs a neutron and is converted into the compound nucleus of uranium-236, which fissions instantaneously.

There are more than 40 different ways a uranium-235 nuclei may fission, resulting in more than 80 different fission products. For the purpose of this discussion, let us consider the most probable fission of a uranium-235 nucleus. In slightly more than 6 percent of the fissions, the uranium-235 nucleus will split into fragments having mass numbers of 95 and 139.

The following equation is typical:

$$^{235}_{92}U + {}^{1}_{0}n \longrightarrow {}^{95}_{39}Y + {}^{139}_{53}I + 2\ {}^{1}_{0}n + \tau,$$

where the daughter products, yttrium and iodine, are both radioactive and decay through beta emission to the stable isotopes of molybdenum ($^{95}_{42}Mo$) and lanthanum ($^{139}_{57}La$) respectively.

One method of determining the energy released from the above reaction is to find the difference in atomic mass units of the daughter products and the original nucleus. It is also necessary that we account for the neutron used to bombard the uranium-235 atom and the two neutrons liberated in the fission process. In the investigation of energy released in this reaction, we find:

Mass of uranium-235 atom	= 235. 04393 amu
Mass of neutron	= 1. 00866 amu
Original mass	= 236. 05259 amu
Mass of molybdenum-95 atom	= 94.90584 amu
Mass of lanthanum-139 atom	= 138.906346 amu
Mass of 2 neutrons	= 2.01732 amu
Total mass of fission fragments	= 235. 8295 amu
Mass defect	= 236. 05259 - 235.8295
	= 0. 22309 amu/fission

Hence,

$$0.22309 \text{ amu/fission} \times 931 \text{ MeV/amu}$$
$$207.7 \text{ MeV/fission}$$

From each fission approximately 200 MeV of energy is released, most of which (about 80 percent) appears immediately as kinetic energy of the fission fragments. As the fission fragments slow down, they collide with other atoms and molecules; this results in a transfer of velocity to the surrounding particles. The increased molecular motion is manifested as sensible heat. The remaining energy is realized from the decay of fission fragments by beta particle and gamma ray emission, kinetic energy of fission neutrons, and instantaneous gamma ray energy.

In a nuclear reactor, the two neutrons liberated in the above reaction are available, under certain conditions, to fission other uranium atoms and assist in maintaining the reactor *critical*. A nuclear reactor is said to be critical if the neutron flux remains constant. *Neutron flux* is defined as the number of neutrons passing through unit area in unit time. A neutron flux of 10^{13} neutrons per square centimeter per second is not uncommon. If the neutron flux is decreasing, the reactor is said to be subcritical; conversely, a reactor is supercritical if the neutron flux is increasing.

Neutron Reactions

Neutrons may be classified by their energy levels. A *fast neutron* has an energy level of greater than 0.1 MeV, an *intermediate neutron* in the process of slowing down possesses an energy level between 1 eV and 0.1 MeV, a *thermal neutron* is in thermal equilibrium with its surroundings and has kinetic energy of less than 1 eV.

Neutrons lose their kinetic energy by interacting with atoms in the surrounding area. The probability of a neutron interacting with one atom is dependent upon the target area presented by that atom for a neutron reaction. This target area (which is the probability of a neutron reaction occurring) is called *cross section*. The unit of cross section measurement is barns. The size of a barn is 10^{-24} square centimeters. Four of the different cross sections that an element may have for neutron processes are as follows:

Scattering cross section is a measure of the probability of an elastic (billiard ball) collision with a neutron. In this type of collision, part of the kinetic energy of the neutron is imparted to the atom and the neutron rebounds after collision. Neutrons are thermalized (reduced to an energy level below 1 eV) by elastic collisions.

Capture cross section is a measure of the probability of the neutron being captured without causing fission.

Fission cross section is a measure of the probability of fission of the atom after neutron capture.

Absorption cross section is a measure of the probability that an atom will absorb a neutron. The absorption cross section is the sum of the capture cross section and the fission cross section.

The cross section for any given element may vary with the energy level of the approaching neutron. In the case of uranium-235, the absorption cross section for a thermal neutron is 100 times the cross section for a fast neutron.

Reactor Principles

A nuclear reactor must contain a *critical mass*. A critical mass contains sufficient fissionable material to enable the reactor to maintain a self-sustaining chain reaction, thereby keeping the reactor critical. A critical mass is dependent upon the species of fissionable material, its concentration and purity the geometry and size of the reactor, and the matter surrounding the fissionable material."

Reactor Fuels

The form and composition of a reactor fuel may vary both in design and in the fissionable isotope used. Many commercial power reactors use a solid fuel element fabricated in plate form, with the fissionable material being enriched uranium in combination with aluminum, zirconium, or stainless steel. Fuel elements may be arranged in thin sandwich layers. This construction provides a relatively large heat transfer area between the fuel elements and the reactor coolant.

The outer cladding on the fuel elements confines the fission fragments within the fuel elements and serves as a heat transfer surface. Cladding materials should be resistant to corrosion, should be able to withstand high temperatures, and should have a small cross section for neutron capture. Three common cladding materials are aluminum, zirconium, and stainless steel. The fuel elements may be assembled in groups, some of which may contain control rods. Several groups of fuel elements placed within a reactor vessel make up the reactor core. It is not necessary that all fuel groups within the reactor contain control rods.

Control Rods

Control rods serve a dual purpose in a reactor. They keep the neutron density (neutron flux) constant within a critical reactor and they provide a means of shutting down the reactor.

The material for a control rod must have a high capture cross section for neutrons and a low fission cross section. Three materials suitable for control rod fabrication are cadmium, boron, and hafnium. Hafnium is particularly suitable for control rods because it has a relatively high capture cross section and because several daughter products after neutron capture are stable isotopes, which also have good capture cross sections.

The control rods are withdrawn from the reactor core until criticality is obtained; thereafter very little movement is required. It is important to note at this point that after criticality is reached, movement of control rods does *not* control the power output of the reactor; it controls only the temperature of the reactor.

Control rod drive mechanisms are so designed that, should an emergency shutdown of the reactor be required, the control rods may be inserted in the core very rapidly. A shutdown of this type is called a *scram*.

Moderators

A moderator is the material used to thermalize the neutrons in a reactor. As previously stated, neutrons are thermalized by elastic collisions; therefore, a good moderator must have a high scattering cross section and a low absorption cross section to reduce the speed of a neutron in a small number of collisions. Nuclei whose mass is close to that of a neutron are the most effective in slowing the neutron; therefore, atoms of low atomic weight generally make the best moderators.

Materials, which have been used as moderators, include light and heavy water, graphite, and beryllium.

Ordinary light water makes a good moderator since the cost is low; however, it must be free from impurities that may capture the neutrons or add to the radiological hazards.

Reactor Coolants

The primary purpose of a reactor coolant is to absorb heat from the reactor. The coolant may be either a gas or a liquid; it must possess good heat transfer properties, have good thermal properties, be noncorrosive to the system, be nonhazardous if exposed to radiation, and be of low cost. Coolants, which have been used in operational and experimental reactors, include light and heavy water, liquid sodium, and carbon dioxide.

Reflectors

In a reactor of finite size, the leakage of neutrons from the core becomes somewhat of a problem. To minimize the leakage, a reflector is used to assist in keeping the neutrons in the reactor. The use of a reflector reduces both the required size of the reactor and the radiation hazards of escaping neutrons. The characteristics required for a reflector are essentially the same as those required for a moderator.

Since ordinary water of high purity is suitable for moderators, coolants, and reflectors, the inference is that it could serve all three functions in the same reactor. This is indeed the case in many nuclear reactors.

Shielding

The shielding of a nuclear reactor serves the dual purpose of (1) reducing the radiation so that it will not interfere with the necessary instrumentation, and (2) protecting operating personnel from radiation.

The type of shielding material used is dependent upon the purpose of the particular reactor and upon the nature of the radioactive particles being attenuated or absorbed.

The shielding against alpha particles is a relatively simple matter. Since an alpha particle has a positive electrical charge of 2, a few centimeters of air is all that is required for attenuation. Any light material such as aluminum or plastics makes a suitable shield for beta particles.

Neutrons and gamma rays have considerable penetrating power; therefore, shielding against them is more difficult. Since neutrons are best attenuated by elastic collisions, any hydrogenous material such as polyethylene or water is suitable as a neutron shield. Sometimes polyethylene with boron is used for neutron shields, as boron has a high neutron capture cross section. A dense material such as lead best attenuates gamma rays.

Nuclear Reactors

The purpose of any power reactor is to provide thermal energy that can be converted to useful work. Several types of experimental and operational reactors have been designed. They include the pressurized water reactor (PWR), the sodium cooled reactor (SCR), the experimental boiling water reactor (BWR), the experimental breeder reactor (BR), and the then experimental gas-cooled reactor (GCR).

The first full-scale nuclear-powered central station in the United States was the pressurized water reactor (PWR) at Shippingport, Pennsylvania. The Shippingport PWR was a thermal, heterogeneous reactor fueled with enriched uranium-235 "seed assemblies" arranged in a square annulus in the center of the core, surrounded by "blanket assemblies" of uranium-238 fuel elements. The PWR reactor and core was called a *converter*, since the uranium-238 was converted into the fissionable fuel of plutonium-239.

The reactor plant consists of a single reactor with four main coolant loops; the plant is capable of maintaining full power on three loops. Each coolant loop contains a steam generator, a pump, and associated piping.

High purity water at a pressure of 2,000 psia serves as both moderator and coolant for the plant. At full power, the inlet water temperature to the reactor is 508° F and the outlet temperature is 542° F.

The coolant enters the bottom of the reactor vessel where 90 percent of the water flows upward between the fuel plates, with the remainder bypassing the core in order to cool the walls of the reactor vessel and the thermal shield. After having absorbed heat as it goes through the core, the water leaves the top of the reactor vessel through the outlet nozzles and flows through connecting piping to the steam generator.

The steam generator is a shell-and-tube type of heat exchanger with the primary coolant (reactor coolant) flowing through the tubes and the secondary water (boiler water) surrounding the tubes. Heat is transferred to the secondary water in the steam generator, producing high quality saturated steam for the use in the turbines.

The primary coolant flows from the steam generator to a hermetically sealed (canned rotor) pump and is pumped through connecting piping to the bottom of the reactor vessel to complete the primary coolant cycle. The pressure on the reactor vessel and the main coolant loop is maintained by a pressurizing tank, which operates under the saturation conditions of 636° F and 2,000 psia. A second function of the pressurizing tank is to act as a surge tank for the primary system. Under no load conditions the inlet, outlet, and average temperatures of the reactor coolant are nearly equal in value. As the power increases, the average temperature remains constant but the inlet and outlet temperatures diverge. Since the colder leg of the primary coolant is the longer, the net effect in the pressurizer is a decrease in level to make up for the increase in density of the water in the primary loop. The reverse holds true with a decreasing power level. Electrical heaters and a spray valve with a supply of water from the cold leg of the primary coolant assist in maintaining a steam blanket in the upper part of the pressurizer and assist in maintaining saturation conditions of 2,000 psia and 636° F.

Principles of Reactor Control

Reactor control principles, which are of particular interest to this discussion, include the *negative temperature coefficient*, the *delayed neutron action*, and the *poisoning* of fuel.

The term "negative temperature coefficient" is used to express the relationship between temperature and reactivity—as the temperature decreases, the reactivity increases. The negative temperature coefficient is a design requirement and is achieved by the proper ratio of elements in the reactor, the geometry of the reactor, and the physical size of the reactor. The negative temperature coefficient makes it possible to keep a power reactor critical with minimum movement of the control rods.

The concept of negative temperature coefficient may be most easily understood by use of an example. Assume that, in the PWR plant, the reactor is critical and the machinery is operating at a given power level. Now, if the valve is opened to increase the turbine speed, the rate of steam flow, and the power level of the reactor, the measurable effect with installed instrumentation is a decrease in the temperature of the primary coolant leaving the steam generator. The decrease in temperature is small but significant in that it results in an increase in density of the coolant. As the density of the coolant increases, so does the magnitude of the neutron scattering cross section. The higher value of the scattering cross section allows the coolant, in its capacity as moderator, to thermalize neutrons at faster rate, supplying more thermal neutrons to be absorbed in the fuel. As more neutrons are absorbed in the fuel, more fissions occur, resulting in a higher power level and more heat being generated by the reactor. The additional heat is removed by the reactor coolant to the secondary water in the steam generator to compensate for the increased steam demand by the turbine. The temperature of the primary coolant leaving the steam generator increases slightly, lowering the scattering cross section of the moderator, and the reactor settles out at a higher power level.

The delayed neutron action is a phenomenon that simplifies reactor control considerably. Each fission in a nuclear reactor releases on the average between two and three neutrons, which either leak out of the reactor or are absorbed in reactor materials. If the reactor material, which absorbs the neutron, happens to be the fissionable fuel, and if the neutron is of proper energy level, another fission is likely to result. The majority of the neutrons released in the fission process appears instantaneously and are termed *prompt neutrons*; but other neutrons are born after fission and are termed *delayed neutrons*. The delayed neutrons appear in a time range of seconds to 3 or more minutes after the fission takes place. The weighted mean lifetime of the delayed neutrons is approximately 12 seconds. About 0.75 percent of the neutrons produced in the fission process are delayed neutrons.

Should a reactor become *prompt critical* (critical on prompt neutrons), it would be very difficult to control and any delayed neutrons would tend to make it supercritical. The delayed neutrons have the effect of increasing the *reactor period* sufficiently to permit reactor control. Reactor period is the time required to change the power level by a factor of e (the base of the system of natural logarithms).

A nuclear *poison* is material in the reactor that has a high absorption cross section for neutrons. Some poisons are classed as burnable poisons and are placed in the reactor for the purpose of extending the core life; other poisons are generated in the fission process and have a tendency to be a hindrance to reactor operation.

A burnable poison has a relatively high cross section for neutron absorption but is used up in the early part of the core life. By adding a burnable poison to the reactor, more fuel can be loaded into the core, thus extending the life of the core.

Most of the fission products produced in a reactor have a small absorption cross section. The most important one that does have a high absorption cross section for neutrons is xenon-135; this can become a problem near the end of core life. Xenon-135 is a direct fission product a small percentage of the time but is mostly produced in the decay of iodine-135 as indicated in the following decay chain:

$$^{135}_{53}I \quad \xrightarrow{\text{6.585 hrs}} \quad ^{135}_{54}Xe \quad \xrightarrow{\text{9.10 hrs}}$$

$$^{135}_{55}Cs \quad \xrightarrow{\text{3} \times 10^6 \text{ yrs}} \quad ^{135}_{56}Ba$$

Xenon-135 has a high neutron absorption cross section. In normal operation of the reactor, xenon-135 absorbs a neutron and is transformed to the stable isotope of xenon-136, which presents no poison problem to the reactor. Equilibrium xenon is reached after about 40 hours of steady-state operation. At this point, the same amount of xenon-135 is being "burned" by neutron absorption as is being produced by the fission process.

The second, and perhaps the more serious, effect of xenon poisoning occurs near the end of core life. As indicated by the half- lives shown in the xenon decay chain, xenon-135 is produced at a faster rate than it decays. The buildup of xenon-135 in the reactor reaches a maximum about 11 hours after shutdown. Should a scram occur near the end of core life, the xenon buildup might make it impossible to take the reactor critical until the xenon has decayed off. In a situation of this type, the reactor may have to sit idle for as much as two days before it is capable of overriding the poison buildup.

The Naval Nuclear Power Plant

Since many aspects of the design and operation of naval nuclear propulsion plants involve classified information, the information presented here is necessarily brief and general in nature.

In a nuclear power plant designed for ship propulsion, weight and space limitations and other factors must be taken into consideration in addition to the factors involved in the design of a shore-based power plant.

The thermodynamic cycle of the shipboard nuclear propulsion plant is similar to that of the conventional steam turbine propulsion plant.

Instead of a boiler, however, the nuclear propulsion plant utilizes a pressurized water reactor as the heat source and a steam generator as a heat exchanger to generate the steam used to drive the propulsion turbines.

The steam generator is a heat exchanger in which the primary coolant transfers heat to the secondary system (boiler water) by conduction. The water in the secondary side of the steam generator, being at lower pressure, changes from the physical state of water to the physical state of steam. This steam then flow through piping to the engine-room.

The engine-room equipment consists of propulsion turbines, turbo-generators, condensers, and associated auxiliaries.

Problems of Nuclear Power

Although many developmental and engineering problems associated with nuclear power have been solved to some extent, some problems remain. A few problems that are of particular importance in connection with the shipboard nuclear power plant are noted here briefly.

The remote possibility of radiological hazards exists even though the radiation is well contained in the shipboard nuclear reactor. To eliminate or minimize the radiological hazards, a high degree of quality control is essential in the design, construction, and operation of nuclear power plants. The high-pressures and temperatures used in nuclear reactors, together with the prolonged periods of continuous operation, pose materials problems. For shipboard use, the great weight of the materials required for shielding presents still other problems.

Although many of these problems may be solved by further technological developments, the problems involved in the selection and training of personnel for nuclear ships appear to be continuing ones. The safe and efficient operation of a shipboard nuclear plant requires highly skilled, responsible personnel who have been thoroughly trained in both the academic and the practical aspects of nuclear propulsion. The selection and training of such personnel is inevitably costly in terms of time and money.

A Look Ahead

New developments in naval engineering tend to be closely related to concepts of strategy. In some instances, new concepts of strategy may force the development of new engineering equipment and plants to meet specific needs; in other instances, the development of a new source of power, a new engine, a new hull form, or a new propulsive device opens up new strategic possibilities.

In previous chapters of this text, we have been concerned with naval engineering plants installed in naval ships from 1955 through 1990. However, it would be unreasonable to assume that achievements from that era as well as present, impressive though they may be, are the last word in naval engineering. Practically everything in the Navy—policies, procedures, publications, systems, and equipment—is subject to rapid change and development, and naval engineering is certainly no exception. The rate of change in technological areas is increasing all the time. The officer who is just beginning his or her naval career may see more innovative changes in naval engineering than have been seen in the past half-century or more. Difficult though it may be, every naval officer has a responsibility for keeping up with new developments.

Because of the increasingly rapid rate of technological development, it is no mean feat to keep abreast of changes in engineering equipment. In order to keep up with new developments in naval engineering, it is necessary to read widely in the literature of the field and to develop a special kind of alertness for information that may ultimately have an effect on naval engineering.

Propulsion Plant Efficiency

As mentioned in Chapter 2, the military value of a naval ship depends largely on its cruising radius, which depends upon the efficiency with which a propulsion plant is operated. Economical operation involves making fuel, lubricating oil, boiler feed water, potable water, and consumable supplies last as long as possible. A ship is not ready for wartime steaming unless the engineering department can and does operate reliably and efficiently. Therefore, it is important that engineering personnel maintain propulsion equipment in a reliable condition and that the equipment be operated at maximum efficiency.

The primary purpose of the peacetime Navy is to train and prepare personnel for wartime conditions. However, in peacetime, maximum economy must be practiced to keep operating and maintenance costs at a minimum.

Accurate knowledge and continuous effort are required to keep propulsion plants operating reliably and efficiently. It is necessary for the personnel concerned to be familiar with the chapters of the *Naval Ships' Technical Manual* that deal with main propulsion plants and associated auxiliary equipment. It is also necessary for personnel to have an accurate knowledge of the appropriate manufacturer's technical manuals, official publications, and directives on operational procedures and material upkeep.

Engineering Reliability

A ship must be capable of performing any duty for which it was designed. A ship is considered reliable when it meets all scheduled operations and is in a position to accept unscheduled tasks. In order to do this, the ship's machinery must be kept in good condition so that the various units will operate as designed. Some of the steps to promote reliability are as follows:

1. A good preventive maintenance program must be carried out at all times. This involves regular tests, inspections, and repairs.
2. Machinery and piping systems must be operated in accordance with good engineering practices. Operating instructions and safety precautions should be posted for each unit of machinery.
3. Supervisory personnel must have a thorough knowledge of the ship's machinery and piping systems. Information on construction, operation, maintenance, and repair of machinery can be obtained from the manufacturer's technical manuals and blueprints.
4. A good engineering department administrative organization will ensure proper assignment of duties and responsibilities and proper training and supervision of personnel.
5. Personnel must be thoroughly trained. This can best be accomplished by a combination of methods. An effective method of training is to have the students learn by doing; a good example of this is watch standing. Another method of training is carrying out regularly scheduled and well-planned instruction periods. These instruction periods are not limited to classroom instruction—they may be conducted by holding engineering casualty control drills while underway.

The Personnel Qualification Standards provide the minimum requirements necessary to qualify on a watch station.

Good engineering practices and safe operation of the plant should never be violated in the interest of economy. Proper operation and maintenance of the engineering plant cannot be overemphasized. Unless a well-trained crew keeps the engineering plant in top operating condition, the ship may not be able to respond adequately to operational requirements.

Altogether, we may expect the future to bring at least a few surprises, a few practical results from ideas which at the moment might appear to be exotic if not downright ludicrous. There these ideas will probably find application in the field of naval engineering, and some of these ideas will doubtless find application in the innovation of propulsion plants of the future.

Index

N

P

R

S

T